P9-DEV-978

Caroline Herschel
*Astronomer and Cataloger
of the Sky*

 Cavendish
Square

New York

Kevin McCombs

Published in 2017 by Cavendish Square Publishing, LLC
243 5th Avenue, Suite 136, New York, NY 10016
Copyright © 2017 by Cavendish Square Publishing, LLC

First Edition

This publication represents the opinions and views of the author based on his or her personal
experience, knowledge, and research. The information in this book serves as a general guide
only. The author and publisher have used their best efforts in preparing this book and disclaim
liability rising directly or indirectly from the use and application of this book.

CPSIA Compliance Information: Batch #CW17CSQ

All websites were available and accurate when this book was sent to press.

Library of Congress Cataloging-in- Publication Data

Names: McCombs, Kevin.
Title: Caroline Herschel: astronomer and cataloger of the sky / Kevin McCombs.
Description: New York : Cavendish Square Publishing, 2017. | Series: Women in science |
Includes index.
Identifiers: ISBN 9781502623171 (library bound) | ISBN 9781502623188 (ebook)
Subjects: LCSH: Herschel, Caroline Lucretia, 1750-1848--Juvenile literature. | Women
astronomers--Great Britain--Biography--Juvenile literature. | Astronomers--Great Britain--
Biography--Juvenile literature. | Women scientists--Great Britain--Biography--Juvenile literature.
Classification: LCC QB36.H5978 M3765 2017 | DDC 520.92--dc23

Editorial Director: David McNamara
Editor: Elizabeth Schmermund
Copy Editor: Rebecca Rohan
Associate Art Director: Amy Greenan
Designer: Ellina Litmanovich
Production Coordinator: Karol Szymczuk
Photo Research: J8 Media

Printed in the United States of America

CONTENTS

A woman uses a modern reflecting telescope on a night full of stars.

INTRODUCTION

WOMEN IN ASTRONOMY

Astronomy is a branch of science open to all who wish to gaze upon a clear night's sky. The field is characterized by observations over time of celestial bodies and their relationships to one another. Astronomers set out to investigate the movements of planets, stars, and **nebulae**. From these observed patterns and characteristics, scientists in this field have uncovered a wealth of knowledge about the physical and chemical nature of heavenly bodies. It is from these observations that we can understand more about our own planet and its position in this vast solar system.

While the practice of observing the stars with the naked eye is accessible to many of us on Earth, it has historically been a select few that have claimed the title of astronomer. To this day, the vast majority of all the astronomers who ever lived were men. Due to the exclusionary nature of academic science, women have faced a number of obstacles to being recognized as astronomers in the public eye. In spite of this fact, the relatively small number of women in this

Caroline Herschel excelled in discovering comets in her observations.

field has contributed an has contributed immensely to astronomical inquiry. In many cases without formal education, women in astronomy had to rely upon their self-determination and passion to lead them to breakthroughs.

In the eighteenth and nineteenth centuries, a number of women contributed to the field of the observed celestial bodies. Caroline Herschel, in particular, helped shape the fundamental observational process of astronomy for generations to come. Her many accomplishments in astronomy are underscored by the hardship she went through as a woman growing up in the eighteenth century. Against all odds, she made a tremendous number of discoveries, which resulted in Herschel receiving some of astronomy's most prestigious awards.

Herschel was one of many astronomers in her family, and she spent much of her life working alongside her brother, William. Together, the two of them set a new standard for optical technologies and their implementation. The Herschel siblings set out to scan the sky in a way that was exact and methodical, revealing all that could be seen with the telescopes of the day. This process of innovation resulted in countless additions to the catalogues of known celestial bodies, pushing the limits of scientific understanding in astronomy. This hard astronomical labor laid the groundwork for many future observers in the field, including future generations of the Herschel family.

The legacy of Caroline Herschel is one of passion, hard work, and humility. From humble beginnings, she conquered the limitations set upon women in science, becoming the first woman ever to publish an astronomical discovery. From this point, she would go on to break records and boundaries throughout her entire career. Her work has inspired a number of women in astronomy since her discoveries over two hundred years ago. As a result, the field of astronomy has seen the rise of brilliant women, whether working as comet hunters, stargazers, or investigators of the deepest mysteries of space.

Caroline and William Herschel conducting astronomical observations with a large telescope.

CHAPTER ONE

EARLY LIFE AND EDUCATION

Caroline Herschel was a woman whose passions and talents brought her to the farthest reaches of the cosmos. She is known for greatly expanding the catalogue of known celestial bodies in the universe during her long life. With such a celebrated career, however, Caroline's upbringing stands in stark contrast to her accomplishments. She was born on March 16, 1750, to father Isaac and mother Anna in Hanover, Germany. Isaac, a musician, performed as the bandmaster of his regiment in the Prussian Army. Her mother Anna was illiterate and took care of the house and children in Isaac's frequent absences. Caroline's brothers were all trained from a very young age to be musicians like their father. As a family of musicians, they lived within modest means.

Herschel's childhood was characterized by hardship, repression, and poor health. As the fifth of six children in the Herschel household, Caroline was relegated to housework and drudgery at a young age instead of to formal education. Anna Herschel believed that it was Caroline's role as the youngest daughter to be a house servant. This meant she opposed even a basic education for her youngest daughter. Isaac had trained every other one of his children, besides Caroline, in reading, arithmetic, and music. Caroline grew up watching her siblings practice to become professional musicians themselves, building careers in the Hanover court orchestra and beyond.

To make matters worse, Caroline contracted smallpox at the age of three. This affliction permanently disfigured her face, leaving scars and causing her left eye to droop. Then, at the age of ten, Caroline suffered a bout of typhus, which stunted her growth, preventing her from growing taller than four feet three inches. For young girls in the eighteenth century, marriage was often stressed as the most important aspect of a woman's life. For Caroline, her family told her frequently that she'd never marry due to her physical appearance. This gave her a very grim outlook on life, even at a young age. Caroline's life in Hanover was practically defined by the physical, mental, and societal limitations that had been placed on her.

While her brothers practiced their instruments and musical composition skills, Caroline was relegated to knitting stockings for the whole family. She was sent to a knitting school for a few hours a day to be able to provide for her parents and siblings. In addition, Caroline had been tasked with writing letters for her illiterate mother as well as a number of women in town. At the beginning of the eighteenth century, it was rare for women to be taught to read or write. As a result, wives in the community needed Caroline to assist them in penning letters to their husbands at war. While this, no doubt, contributed to the macabre atmosphere of her upbringing, it also allowed Caroline the opportunity to become a skilled writer.

During this period in time, the Seven Years' War dominated the lives of many Europeans. Isaac Herschel enlisted in the military

A group of eighteenth-century musicians perform for members of German high society.

marching band. His departure cast great shadows over the whole family, as Isaac had previously been injured while in battle. In the battle of Dettingen in 1743, Isaac and his regiment had endured harsh weather conditions. During a particularly heavy night of rain, the bandmaster was positioned in a cold, wet trench until the following morning. These extreme conditions resulted in Isaac not being able to use his limbs for a long period of time. While he eventually recovered his motor skills, Isaac suffered from a weakened constitution and breathing troubles for the rest of his life. This meant that future periods of service came at a great physical price for Isaac Herschel, and his failing health made life very difficult at home.

In Caroline Herschel's memoirs, seemingly all joy or happiness experienced in her childhood was through the enjoyment of her brothers' accomplishments. She lived vicariously through the happiness found by the men of the family through music and philosophy. In her memoirs, Caroline writes:

❝ *My brothers were often introduced as solo performers and assistants in the orchestra of the court, and I remember that I was frequently prevented from going to sleep by the lively criticism on music on coming from a concert, or conversations on philosophical subjects which lasted frequently till morning, in which my father was a lively partaker and assistant of my brother William by contriving self-made instruments ... Often I would keep myself awake that I might listen to their animating remarks, for it made me so happy to see them so happy.* **❞**

While she was directly excluded from engaging in such conversations (mostly because they carried on long after her bedtime), Caroline showed a genuine interest for the family's enriching dialogues. She took every opportunity she could to glean knowledge from passing debates on thinkers like Gottfried Wilhelm Leibnitz and Isaac Newton. Caroline cherished what little opportunity she had for intellectual stimulation, which appeared to have a profound impact on her eventual career. In a particularly important passage of her memoir, Caroline wrote:

> **❝** *My father was a great admirer of astronomy, and had some knowledge of that science; for I remember his taking me, on a clear frosty night, into the street, to make me acquainted with several of the most beautiful constellations, after we had been gazing at a comet which was then visible. And I well remember with what delight he used to assist my brother William in his various contrivances in the pursuit of his philosophical studies, among which was a nearly turned 4-inch [10.16-centimeter] globe, upon which the equator and ecliptic were engraved by my brother.* **❞**

This passage is noteworthy in Caroline's life for a great number of reasons. This was not only one of the first instances of her contact with the study of astronomy, but it shows her fondness for seeing the beauty of the night sky. More important still was her father's decision to take Caroline to see a visible comet in addition to the usual constellations. Her fascination with comets would continue throughout her life as an astronomer and thinker. Also prominent in this passage is Caroline's intense affection for her brother and his intellectual pursuits.

A globe used for study and astronomical research

Caroline Herschel: Astronomer and Catologer of the Sky

Isaac Herschel sought to give all of his children the best possible experience and education in life. In spite of his wife Anna's discouragement, Isaac would try to make time in between lessons to include Caroline in musical activities. He would often allow her some practice on a violin and would get her to perform as second chair in small family performances. While she never had enough time to become a proficient violinist, Caroline thoroughly enjoyed Isaac's teachings. Even watching him give lessons to other pupils raised her spirits while she knitted in the house.

Isaac worked hard in spite of all his ailments until the day he passed. In August of 1764, he suffered a paralytic seizure, which marked the loss of function on the right side of his body. He never regained his ability to play the violin, although he continued teaching students and copying music until he could no longer leave his bed. In the last three years of his life, Isaac suffered greatly, regretting that he was unable to properly and formally educate his youngest daughter. He died at the age of sixty-one in March 1767, leaving behind a legacy of virtue and hard work for his children. At the age of seventeen, Caroline was devastated by the loss of her father, a profound and sympathetic mentor. This left her with grave uncertainty for her future, for as she put it, she "could not bear the idea of being turned into an Abigail or a housemaid."

By this point, Caroline's brother William was living near London in Bath, England, working as an accomplished musician and composer. His visits to Hanover were usually short, much to Caroline's dismay, as she longed to see her favorite brother. His correspondence with the family in Hanover usually came in the form of letters to his brother Jacob. In these letters, he discussed music theory with his younger brother, making it rather exclusive to the rest of the family and especially

A BROTHER'S HOPE AND INSPIRATION

William Herschel was a famous European musician, composer, and astronomer. With his father's passion for music and stargazing, William quickly made a name for himself playing with instruments both optical and musical. It is this drive and curiosity that defines the Herschel name, as many in their lineage went on to pursue important astronomical work. This strong scientific heritage also comes from a penchant for inspiring others. Early in his astronomical investigations, Sir William Herschel would write letters about his work to his family back in Hanover to involve them in his scientific pursuits.

Caroline invariably cited her brother William as the prime inspiration for her involvement with astronomy. Were it not for the initial interest and opportunity that brought her away from Hanover, it is possible that she would have continued living as the family servant. Instead, William took the time that he could to teach her lessons in music, arithmetic, and optics. By stepping into the role of mentor, William had a profound effect on the rest of his sister's career. While it was their father Isaac who first showed Caroline the constellations in the night sky, it was her loving brother who gave her the first opportunity behind the **eyepiece** of a telescope. By entrusting her with optical equipment, William inspired the curiosities of a budding astronomer in his sister.

to Caroline. In 1771, however, William Herschel sent a letter to his family with an interesting proposal. He offered to bring Caroline to Bath with him so that she could try out as a vocalist in some of his performances and oratorios. By some miracle, Anna accepted the terms of her daughter's departure, under the condition that Caroline must return to Hanover if she did not find success as a vocalist within two years. This would require Jacob to give Caroline singing lessons before she left, a task which Jacob refused, ridiculing his sister and her abilities. Undeterred, Caroline took every waking opportunity to practice when nobody was home. She would even go to the extent of singing while biting down on a gag to reduce her volume during practice. She spent time knitting enough stockings to last the family two years in her absence, just to appease her mother.

When the day finally came on August 16, 1772, Caroline departed for Bath on a six-day excursion in an open **postwagon**. In order to get to England, she had to board a small boat under bleak and stormy conditions. By the end of the trip, the boat was in shambles, and two English sailors dropped her off on the English shore. Traveling again by horse-drawn cart, Caroline and her brother would endure one last mishap on their way to Bath as the horse suddenly ran away, flipping the cart and its passengers into a ditch. They were miraculously uninjured and finally completed the journey through London.

It was in Bath that Caroline's life finally took a turn for the better. While she arrived under the pretenses of attaining a lifelong career as a vocalist, her time in Bath would take yet another unexpected turn. For while it was William's plan to give his sister lessons in singing, he was at the time very taken with his newfound obsession for astronomy. Every waking hour William had away from conducting large performances was spent in an improvised workshop where he tinkered with optical

Illustration of a post wagon used for extended trips in the eighteenth and nineteenth centuries

instruments. By some serendipitous event, William had picked up a book by Professor Robert Smith called *A Compleat System of Opticks*. This text came to him after reading through Smith's other text on harmonics, which had come, no doubt, from his musical curiosities. Using the knowledge he gained from these two volumes, William began to design and manufacture his own telescopes.

In spite of his avid curiosities, William still wished to help his sister begin a career in singing. He arranged for a woman with whom he was acquainted, named Mrs. Colnbrook, to help his sister. By her good graces, she took Caroline to London for two weeks to hear what truly professional vocalists sounded like. Every night, they attended the opera or the theater, requiring hairdressers and nice clothing with which Caroline had very little experience. To this point, she had been only a poor housemaid in Hanover. These experiences had a profound effect on Caroline's outlook for both music and life. By the time their two weeks had ended, winter was rolling in, making the path home unpassable. She would stay in London for another six weeks, being exposed to the niceties of high society and shaping her talents as a vocalist.

A print of late eighteenth-century women's fashion for the high class

When she finally arrived back in Bath, Caroline found her brother completely immersed in the construction of large telescopes. As an increasing amount of his time was swallowed by his passion for astronomy, William began to need more and more assistance from Caroline for clerical work. Her education in arithmetic at this point was shoddy and required much remediation, which William was happy to provide. It was at this point that Caroline's role as an astronomer's assistant was beginning to come into view. From here, Caroline had no idea of the extent to which she herself would become a celebrated astronomer in her own right.

*A small portion of the visible stars
and nebulae on a clear night.*

CHAPTER TWO

CAROLINE HERSCHEL'S TIMES

Caroline Herschel's distinguished career developed during the late eighteenth and early nineteenth centuries. During this period, life in England involved heavily imposed roles and expectations within society. Under the rule of the monarch George III, the English empire largely asserted control over its people both at home and abroad in its colonies. This time period saw the rise of the American Revolution as ruling structures became challenged by new ideas. By the same token, challenges were being made to fundamental assertions in human understanding through the lens of science. Scientific revolutions began to take hold in the wake of great discoveries. These centuries placed greater emphasis on the study of **empirical** data. This means that scientific hypotheses would be tested more strictly through observation instead of through beliefs or philosophical stances.

One group of people in particular dominated the scientific work at this time: men of high stature. As Herschel would go on to show, this domination was largely the result of imposed societal norms and gender roles, with very little to do with the talents or ambitions of women interested in scientific fields. That being said, Herschel managed to become a prominent astronomer through a combination of favorable circumstances, rigorous training, and voracious work ethic. Her success as an astronomer sprouted from seemingly unthinkable beginnings given the education she received and the class she was born into. In spite of it all, Herschel took every waking opportunity to procure knowledge and skills that would have never been expected of women at the time.

LIFE AS AN ASSISTANT ASTRONOMER

When Herschel returned from her vocal training in London, she found herself immediately immersed in her new passion—not for music, but for astronomy. Her brother William no longer focused on a career as a composer and conductor, instead spending his evenings constructing optical devices with which to study the heavens. As time went by, William would require increasingly more of Caroline's talents as a scribe or account manager. Her previous experience managing the Herschel household began to take on a new light as Caroline's clerical duties transformed from writing mere letters for her mother, to documenting nightly discoveries of celestial bodies. Moreover, Caroline began to take the findings of previous nights and consolidate them into rudimentary catalogues and academic papers for William.

What began as a nighttime obsession became far more serious for William Herschel upon his discovery of the planet Uranus. A paper submitted to the **Royal Astronomical Society** on the subject garnered much attention and admiration for the rising astronomer. In fact, this particular discovery caught the eye of King George III himself, who demanded that William bring one of his new telescopes to the royal observatory. With William's advancements in optical technologies, he was able to show the King his new discoveries where other telescopes of the time fell short. This resulted in William's appointment as Court Astronomer. Shortly thereafter, William abandoned his career in music entirely to fulfill his role as a scientist. With this transition of careers, however, came far greater expectations of Caroline's time as an assistant.

This pivotal moment would mean the end of Herschel's career as a singer almost as quickly as it began. Immediately, the siblings uprooted to Datchet, England, and began working on telescopes in the hunt for a comprehensive inventory of the sky. From a very young age, Herschel had been raised to serve the good of her family without taking pride or interest in her own pursuits. This meant that she identified her position in life as peripheral to the curiosities of her brother. While this move would prove paramount in her development as an astronomer, it truly shows the impact that societal pressures had on her self-image, which could be described as "humble" at best.

Under the employment of the king, William began construction on a series of large twenty-foot telescopes. The size and scope of this project required the labor of an entire local community of craftsmen. Both day and night, workers toiled casting lenses, polishing mirrors for **reflectors**, and manufacturing the great tubes of the telescopes. Caroline, at this time, did any and all work that needed to be done. This meant that she would spend an occasional evening grinding and polishing mirrors herself to complete the job. The management of this number of workers, however, proved to be a formidable endeavor in and of itself.

THE DISCOVERY OF URANUS

William Herschel's discovery of the planet Uranus undoubtedly changed the course of both his and his sister's lives. Given that scientific grants were handed out by the monarchy at the time, the favor of the king was paramount for advancement in some fields. In this case, astronomy of the time required a significant amount of resources to achieve breakthroughs in technology. Due to the fact that reflecting telescopes were so recently invented, engineers needed to research and develop the technology to actually turn them into practical devices. This meant that the Herschels needed access to entire crews of people to construct telescopes that had never been imagined, using resources provided by the crown.

Caroline benefited greatly from this discovery, as it allowed her the opportunity to work with the most advanced telescopes of the time. As a sibling duo, the Herschels were able to document uncharted territory in space. This inspired Caroline's investigations to a great degree as she learned more every day as an assistant. The methodical documentation of her observations of the night sky provided her with a framework to make her own discoveries, which she used to great effect. In essence, the discovery of the planet Uranus set off a chain reaction of events, which then allowed for a lifetime of astronomical labor. The funding provided by the king made their contributions to astronomy possible as they were provided with greater and greater resources. The ability to clearly see objects hidden to less sophisticated telescopes put the Herschels a cut above the rest.

With William out on missions to gather construction materials and consult with other academics, Caroline was often left to oversee operations. The fabrication process took over every part of the house that was available. This included sections of the library where important records and documents were kept. The disarray of construction required a great deal of organization and coordination on the part of Caroline who needed, at one point, to salvage important texts from the destructive force of workmen. In her memoirs, Herschel recalls the chaos of this period, lamenting the workers' carelessness and thievery.

> *For at last everything that could be carried away was gone, and nothing but rubbish left. Even tables for the use of workrooms vanished: one in particular I remember, the drawer of which was filled was slips of experiments made on the rays of light and heat, was lost out of the room in which the women had been ironing. This could not but produce the greatest disorder and inconvenience in the library and in the room into which the apparatus for observing had been moved, when the observatory was wanted for some other purpose; they were at last so encumbered by stores and tools of all sorts that no room for a desk or an Atlas remained. It required my utmost exertion to rescue the manuscripts in hand from destruction by falling into unhallowed hands or being devoured by mice.*

Without her diligence during this time, astronomy may well have lost precious documents of hypotheses and observations. Even in the early stages of her training as an astronomer's assistant, Herschel

Caroline Herschel.

Caroline and William Herschel polishing mirrors for a new telescope.

carried with her a sense of personal responsibility for astronomical endeavors. She spent this period working at a feverish pace to ensure that the checkbooks were balanced and the house remained whole in spite of disorder. As a result, she was largely responsible for the success of the operation, making sure that her brother's engineering fantasies came to fruition. The construction of these twenty-foot telescopes would prove to be incredibly important in the astronomical investigations to come.

With the technological advances of the construction phase in Datchet, the Herschels were now capable of putting the new telescopes to good use. The power of this telescope would allow for a project of immense importance and scope. The Herschels set out to scan the heavens in order to vastly increase the number of recorded stars and nebulae for the field of astronomy. As a team, brother and sister would begin a methodical inventory of new discoveries, providing other astronomers with important information to study the characteristics and movement of celestial bodies.

And so the Herschels began their project of epic proportions: to catalog the skies with the best observational tools the world had ever seen. During this period, William spent much time away from home, meeting with academics and royalty, and leaving Caroline to oversee a large part of the operations in Datchet. It would be her job to manage the budget of ongoing projects, take down detailed accounts of nightly observations, and prepare papers for publication by the Royal Astronomical Society.

The Herschels developed a method whereby William sat at his place at the eyepiece while another assistant operated the rope system used to move the telescope as it vertically scanned the sky. This was called "**sweeping**," when the telescope would take methodical inventory of celestial objects through focusing on one strip of the sky at a time.

Once an object was detected, William would ring a bell, signaling to Caroline to open a window and take down the information he shouted to her. These observations were recorded with the utmost haste and precision as the conditions changed rapidly over time. Due to Earth's rotation, the vertical column of a sweep would only feature a certain portion of the sky for a limited amount of time. In essence, the duo had to work quickly enough to outrun the movement of Earth before a new set of stars and nebulae came into view.

For Caroline, this meant she had to keep a highly efficient system for logging data about the observations. She organized her logbooks into columns that visually resembled the sweep of the telescope itself. In these columns, as much information as possible was recorded as to the time and date of the observation, position of the lens, and relation of the object observed to other recorded objects. Her meticulous recordkeeping during this project led quickly to an extensive catalog of 1,000 observations. To date, no other catalog had even half that number of astronomical objects.

These forays into new optical technology, however, came with a significant set of challenges for astronomer and assistant alike. Precisely wielding a twenty-foot telescope tube required large, complex scaffolding and a series of pulleys. During the early stages of this development, William's constructions had relatively little accommodations for operation. This meant that workers had to hoist ropes from pulleys by hand and move the large instrument without the aid of the clever engineering that would be developed in subsequent years. At one point, William wished to take advantage of a clear night's sky in spite of the fact that the reflector had not yet been properly mounted. The ongoing construction around the telescope also meant that the observation area was often riddled with tools and hazards, making for tough working conditions. Caroline suffered greatly in these conditions. In her memoirs, she recounted a terrible accident that occurred due to these hazards:

> [By] about 10 o'clock a few stars became visible, and in the greatest hurry all was got ready for observing. My brother at the front of the telescope directing me to make some alteration in the lateral motion which was done by a machinery in which the point of support of the tube and mirror rested … at each end of the machine or trough was an iron hook such as butchers use for hanging their joints upon, and having to run in the dark on ground covered foot deep with melting snow, I fell on one of these hooks which entered my right leg about 6 inches above the knee, my brothers call 'make haste' I could only answer by a pitiful cry 'I am hooked.' He and the workman were instantly with me, but they could not lift me without leaving near 2 oz. of my flesh behind. The workman's wife was called but was afraid to do anything, and I was obliged to be my own surgeon by applying aquabaseda and tying a kerchief about it for some days; till Dr Lind hearing of my accident brought me ointment and lint and told me how to use it. But at the end of six weeks I began to have some fears about my poor limb and had Dr Lind's opinion, who on seeing the wound found it going on well; but said, if a soldier had met with such a hurt he would have been entitled to 6 weeks nursing in a hospital.

Here, Herschel shows the extent of her sacrifice as an astronomer's assistant. What's perhaps most striking about this account is her competency, in spite of her injury, to perform surgery upon herself. This is truly a grim indicator of the time period in which medical emergencies could not always be properly addressed. No doubt, her steady hand while knitting stockings prepared her for such a gruesome task. Herschel, in service to astronomy, put her body on the line to fulfill her role as a faithful assistant. This level of servitude stems heavily from the expectations placed upon women during this time period in England. Her dedication becomes even more apparent, however, when she notes: "I had however the comfort to know that my brother was no loser through this accident for the remainder of the night was cloudy and several nights afterwards afforded only a few short intervals favorable for sweeping until the 16 of January before there was any necessity for exposing myself for a whole night to the severity of the season."

With a kind of morbid humor, Herschel took this opportunity to think only of her brother's work. Her dedication to astronomical pursuits seems to extend beyond the reach of concerns even for her own well-being. In eighteenth century Britain, women were supposed to take on these roles. Society thus played a crucial part in devaluing women's self-perception when pursuing any endeavor beyond the scope of service to others.

During this period of time, William constructed a simple telescope specifically for his sister to begin sweeps of the night sky on her own. This small telescope, though not nearly as accurate as the twenty-foot, was very practical for individual use. With a little bit of training, Caroline began to log her own personal observations and discoveries. This was truly the first step towards surpassing her role of an assistant to become a full-fledged astronomer.

In order to perform these sweeps, Caroline had to become learned in both mathematics and contemporary astronomical catalogs of the day. The frequent absence of her brother made math tutoring sparse, so she took every opportunity during meals to quiz William for information. Additionally, William compiled small lessons for his sister, which she studied intensely. These texts were titled "A Little Geometry for Lina," or "A Little Algebra for Lina," and served as her primary means of education in arithmetic. This was extraordinary for the time period, given that women were seldom taught math at all, much less at the level Herschel eventually gained proficiency. Her studies were largely self directed, serving the purpose of being able to calculate the distances of new objects in the sky from reference points of known stars and nebulae. These calculations involved a large degree of trigonometry, specifically **triangulation**. This mathematical practice provided Herschel with a method to calculate and record the distances of celestial bodies from each other at a given vantage point on Earth. This meant that other astronomers using comparable telescopes could quickly identify her findings using coordinates produced by a combination of trigonometry and the positions of objects known in the astronomical catalogues of the time.

Before being able to identify a star, nebula, or comet, Herschel had to reference John Flamsteed's *Atlas Coelestis*. This work was, at the time, the most comprehensive inventory of celestial bodies and came with its own identification and numbering system for any given, observable entity. In addition, Herschel used French astronomer Charles Messier's list of "objects" that resembled comets. This became increasingly useful in her sweeps as she began to come across a number of yet-unidentified objects in the sky. This work involved great care and precision, methodically moving her instrument in the sky, all the while noting the time and consequent position of Earth's rotation.

Herschel gives an account of these early explorations in her memoirs years later:

> *In my brother's absence from home, I was of course left solely to amuse myself with my own thoughts, which were anything but cheerful. I found I was to be trained for an assistant-astronomer, and by way of encouragement a telescope adapted for 'sweeping,' consisting of a tube with two glasses, such as are commonly used in a 'finder,' was given me. I was 'to sweep for comets,' and I see by my journal that I began August 22nd, 1782, to write down and describe all remarkable experiences I saw in my 'sweeps,' which were horizontal. But it was not till the last two months of the same year that I felt the least encouragement to spend the star-light nights on a grass-plot covered with dew or hoar frost, without a human being near enough to be within call. I knew too little of the real heavens to be able to point out every object so as to find it again without losing too much time by consulting the Atlas.*

In this passage, Herschel takes seemingly every opportunity to belittle her own work. In the absence of her brother, she claims no mastery over her newfound role as an assistant. Despite performing astronomical tasks, Herschel views her work as a series of motions guided only by the talents of her brother. This kind of self-degradation was almost iconic among

Herschel's memoirs and letters, downplaying the significance of her work and her rightful place as a scientist. She continues:

> But all these troubles were removed when I knew my brother to be at no great distance making observations with his various instruments on **double stars**, *planets, [etc.] and I could have his assistance immediately when I found a nebula, or cluster of stars, of which I intended to give a catalog; but at the end of 1783 I had only marked fourteen, when my sweeping was interrupted by being employed to write down my brother's observations with the large twenty-foot [telescope]. I had, however, the comfort to see that my brother was satisfied with my endeavors to assist him when he wanted another person, either to run to the clocks, write down a memorandum, fetch and carry instruments, or measure the ground with poles, etc., of which something of the kind every moment would occur.*

Here, Caroline revels in the opportunity to participate in William's studies and observations. She appears to gain confidence only in the presence of her brother's mastery, deferring to his judgment for any personal finding or documentation. Again, this persistence to diminish her own scientific perspective stands as a filter for her every recollection. In spite of such obvious contribution to her field, Herschel gains satisfaction only in the reflection of her brother's admiration.

Herschel was not only taught to diminish her accomplishments in her study of astronomy. In fact, during Herschel's time training in London, she was taught not only how to sing, but how to present herself as an English woman. This involved a series of constraints, from posture to incessant apology in her speech. During one particular incident, an unnamed woman in Bath scolded Herschel for "being [her] own trumpeter." Moments like these shaped life for women of high society in England in a way that was in no way expected of men. Scientific and academic discovery, for men, was largely considered to be a triumph of the individual during the enlightenment period. Instead, modesty, on the side of self-deprecation was expected of esteemed women. While this indoctrination of gender roles played a part in limiting Herschel's experience, she used her astute understanding of the status quo to ultimately gain favor in the scientific community.

A GREAT DISCOVERY

While William's regular absences seemed, on the one hand, to fill Caroline with dread, they also allowed for a great amount of time behind the eyepiece of the telescope. Herschel used her simple **Newtonian sweeper** to great effect on the night's sky. The more time Herschel spent behind the telescope, the greater her knowledge and comfort with the instrument became. She began to take every cloudless night as an opportunity for diligent work, documenting her findings along the way. While her hard work began paying off almost immediately in the discovery of new nebulae to be cataloged later with William, Caroline made a profound discovery all her own. On August 1, 1786, Herschel sent a letter to a scholar and dear friend of William's about her discovery. This would be the first letter ever written to the Royal Astronomical Society by a woman.

Herschel began the letter with a very careful approach: "In consequence of the Friendship which I know to exist between you and my Brother I venture to trouble you in his absence with the following imperfect account of a comet." Perhaps understanding the importance of such a letter, Herschel penned it with the utmost care and precision, posturing herself upon the well-respected reputation of her brother. Given that the observation of a comet is highly time-sensitive, this matter simply could not wait for William's return on any occasion. As a result, Herschel had to muster the confidence to send a letter that identified herself—a woman—as a contributor to the field of astronomy.

Having performed the duties of scribe for William on a number of academic papers, Caroline had been able to outline a set of instructions to aid another astronomer in seeking out her comet. As part of the scientific method, this allowed her to submit her work for **peer review**, allowing the Royal Society to verify her findings themselves. In her letter, Herschel, using simple trigonometry, then described a process for uniquely identifying the phenomenon she observed. She documented the movement of the comet over the course of multiple hours of study, showing a methodical proof of her process. Herschel also outlined the specifications of the instrument she used to make the observation, so as to provide a reference for attaining similar results. In reality, the society would use far more sophisticated telescopes to confirm her discovery, proving the power of hard work since she had used such a simple instrument.

At both the start and conclusion of the letter, Herschel makes reference to her connection to her brother and his "astronomical friends." Without any such consolation, this letter would have surely sufficed in providing the Society with a new discovery in the field of astronomy. Her knowledge of the perception of women's accomplishments of the time, however, prompted a very poised and hesitant claim to her discovery. As a result, she offered the Royal Society the opportunity to confirm or deny her claim. By doing this, Herschel strove to defend herself against any criticism for her work, from either the Royal Society or from British society at large.

It is important to note that during this time period, women in England were not even awarded academic degrees at universities. In spite of this fact, Herschel stood up to make her first in a series of important contributions alongside the work of men with doctorates and privileged upbringings. Herschel defies the structures of her times, exceeding every expectation of her class and gender during this period. Had her mother's wishes of domesticity been fulfilled, Herschel could have been sentenced to a lifetime of knitting and drudgery. Instead, afforded the opportunities given to her brother and passed along to her, she ascended to a position that would never have been allowed for most women at the time.

Herschel's discovery was truly historic. With this paper, she became the first woman not only to submit a discovery, but to discover an object as highly sought after as a comet. During this time, comets were the subject of much debate and curiosity in astronomical circles. Any and all information as to their whereabouts was of critical importance to the investigation of their nature. While academic and professional circles of the time identified Herschel as a lowly assistant, her contribution to the field speaks for itself. This would be the first of many comets discovered using this sweeping method. No other individual can lay claim to the discoveries she made this way, alone in a quiet field, carefully scanning the night for new objects.

After some time, William's growing esteem as an astronomer and engineer began to open new avenues for his career. Having always dreamed of creating telescopes of, at the time, unthinkable scale,

The famous forty-foot reflecting telescope constructed by the Herschels for astronomical research

William's endeavors were limited by the constraints of his salary. However, the twenty-foot telescope the Herschels had been using to sweep and catalog the sky once again caught the attention of the British monarchy. The telescope was unparalleled in its clarity and reach at the time of its completion. This, however, did not stop William's hunger for the capacities of optical instrumentation. As a result, William was granted the opportunity to construct a massive forty-foot telescope in the name of research for the Royal Society of Astronomers. This meant a big paycheck for William, but an even bigger moment for Caroline and female astronomers in general. Herschel recounts the budget in the following passage of her memoirs:

> In consequence of an application made through Sir J. Banks to the King, my brother had in August a second £2,000 granted for completing the forty-foot, and £200 yearly for the expense of repairs, such as ropes, painting, [etc.] and the keep and clothing of the men who attended at night. A salary of fifty pounds a year was also settled on me as an assistant to my brother, and in October I received twelve pounds ten, being the first quarterly payment of my salary, and the first money I ever in all my lifetime thought myself to be at any liberty to spend to my own liking.

This was truly an historic moment in the advancement of women in science. Never before had the monarchy granted a salary for a female in scientific inquiry, not even as an assistant. It was quite evident from her numerous contributions that Herschel proved herself an integral part of the exploration of the heavens. While her salary still reflected that of an assistant and not the astronomer she had already become, it stands as a testament to the impact of her work.

The royal salary was due to the intersection of a number of positive factors in Herschel's life. Certainly the dedication to her brother and his work stands at the forefront of this accomplishment. William's esteem as a man of science opened a lot of doors for the sibling duo as professional connections looked favorably upon their work and technical advances. The fact that they were siblings no doubt contributed to the perception that Caroline was indispensable to her brother's work. It is upon these premises that Herschel's dedication and practice uniquely qualified her for the position at the time. Therefore, seeing Caroline as a hard-working extension of her brother, the king made an unprecedented decision to employ a woman in the field of science. It goes without saying that other women of the time, no matter how driven or gifted, would not have been afforded such compensation strictly on their own merits.

A Ptolemaic model of the solar system from the first century CE

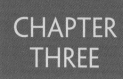

CAROLINE HERSCHEL'S FIELD OF STUDY

The Herschel siblings together made an unprecedented amount of discoveries in the field of observational astronomy. These discoveries contributed to a catalog of work that ancient astronomers began thousands of years before. The history of astronomy reveals an interesting look into the history of human curiosity itself. It explores early peoples' beliefs, observations, and their wonder at the night sky, and how their early explorations shaped our scientific inquiries today. In order to place Caroline Herschel's work in context, this chapter will examine the advancements of astronomical work.

EARLY ASTRONOMY

Astronomy was one of the first sciences to develop in the ancient world due to its predictive power for recurring events. Because the movement of the stars at night could be tracked during clear skies, early astronomers used their observations of the stars to keep track of time. Calendars based on constellations were constructed to help understand the passage of time. Astronomy, as a result, was used largely to identify harvest periods for crops and signify events for rituals and social gatherings.

In the earliest cultures of Mesopotamia, astronomical study was often very similar to what we know today as astrology, or how the movement of celestial bodies in the night's sky affects human behavior and events. While the hypotheses proposed by these systems were largely superstitious or mythical in nature, the practice of observation laid the groundwork for astronomy as a scientific field. The Babylonians devoted entire teams of scribes to record the observed movement of heavenly bodies. In Mesopotamia, the advent of clay tablets played an integral role in the process of recording observations. Due to the fact that celestial events would recur after long periods of time, information had to be kept safe for many years. The tablets could be stored in the security of the Mesopotamian temples so as to avoid damage from moisture. In these collections, broken tablets could simply be recopied onto fresh clay.

BABYLON AND ASTRONOMICAL DIARIES

Over time, Babylonian scribes began to keep nightly records of astronomical observations. These diaries, written in the seventh century BCE, were some of the first records of astronomical projects spanning across years of study. The technological and mathematical limitations of the time resulted in largely inaccurate measurements and observations. For the field of astronomy, however, precision of observation is not the only important factor for predicting astronomical events and cataloging celestial objects. The diligent collection of observational data over time proved to be important in and of itself. With this data, Babylonians were able to predict the movement of the moon and planets based on a series of observed patterns. While these accounts oversimplified the complexity and unpredictability of planetary orbits, they still produced useful information for the Mesopotamians.

The Babylonians would later apply mathematical theories to strengthen their understanding of planetary movement. Each observed planet in the solar system followed its own set of orbital patterns for the astronomers of Babylon. In particular, a planet's **retrograde movement** was important to understand the planet's position in the orbital theater of the cosmos. Retrograde movement is observed when the orbit of a planet reverses from the direction of Earth's rotation about its axis. This occurs naturally based on the difference in orbital cycle between Earth and other planets in the solar system. By using the duration of a planet's observed time in retrograde movement, the Babylonians calculated positions as a number of degrees in a circular orbit. In other words, they gathered observational data that clearly showed that planets moved at various speeds across their cycles. This meant that the astronomers identified patterns where a given planet would traverse greater numbers of degrees in circular orbit for certain intervals of time.

GREEK ASTRONOMY AND GEOMETRIC RELATIONSHIPS

Ancient Greek culture, too, was heavily entwined with the developing science of astronomy. Mythology, philosophy, and mathematics all converged upon the field of astronomy to address a number of pressing questions in ancient Greece. Concerned largely with the nature of the physical world, the Greeks sought to find the shape and size of Earth. The

Greek philosopher Aristotle is thought to have written the first recorded account explaining Earth's spherical shape. Using the observation of a lunar eclipse, Aristotle noted the circular shadow cast across the surface of the moon. Given that a sphere produces a shadow in the shape of a circle when directly between a light source and an opaque surface, Aristotle proved his hypothesis through empirical investigation.

In the third century BCE, the scholar Eratosthenes set up a different experiment to hypothesize about the properties of Earth. Using Greek advancements in the study of geometry, he formulated a method not only to mathematically prove the curvature of the Earth, but to provide the first recorded measurements for the dimensions of the globe. Eratosthenes set up an experiment whereby he noted the shadow cast by a vertical pole in the sand when the sun was directly overhead the Greek city of Syene. Knowing full well that the light from the sun would produce no shadow upon an object parallel to the direction of the light, he used this observation as the control of the experiment.

In a rather tedious project, Eratosthenes enlisted the help of an assistant to record the distance, in steps, on a walk between Syene and the city of Alexandria. With this distance in mind, he traveled to Alexandria to make another observation. At the exact same time of day, Eratosthenes placed another pole upright in the ground and measured the shadow cast by the sunlight. The shadow of the pole on the ground showed that the sunlight was hitting at an angle of about 7.2 degrees. He then proposed that, since the distance between Syene and Alexandria produced a 7.2-degree shift in the angle of the sunlight, this measurement could be used to calculate Earth's circumference. The 7.2-degree angle could be seen as a percentage of the 360-degree total of the spherical shape of Earth.

This text by Nikolaus Copernicus explained his theory of heliocentrism.

Since 360/7.2=50, Eratosthenes simply multiplied the distance between Syene and Alexandria by a factor of 50 to reach the total circumference. His calculation of roughly 28,000 miles is amazingly close to the actual circumference of 24,901 miles.

The Greeks' clever implementation of geometric calculations allowed them to start formulating ideas about the nature of the entire system of planetary motion. In a book entitled *On Speeds,* Greek astronomer and thinker Eudoxus of Cnidus proposed a model in which the solar system moved as a set of circles that shared the same center. This would later be called the **theory of homocentric spheres** and featured Earth at the very center of planetary movement. At the time, the theory explained the observed patterns of planets in retrograde movement. It failed to explain, however, why certain planets appeared brighter, or closer, during different periods in their cycle.

The Eudoxian project would later be abandoned due to its inability to accurately predict the movements of the heavens. In spite of this fact, the crux of Eudoxus's theory remained at the heart of astronomical thinking for well over a thousand years and the model of circular orbits prevailed with a few important additions. In 220 BCE, Apollonius of Perga proposed an amendment to the theory of homocentric spheres by introducing eccentric circles, or circles that do not share the same center but are interlinked. This innovation provided a much better explanation for the observed phenomena that the sun appeared to travel more quickly during the summer at its closest proximity to Earth. The Greeks measured the duration of seasons in relation to the sun's supposed "orbit" in order to strengthen this model. This accomplishment lingered until the seventeenth century, when the **Copernican Revolution** unseated Earth as the center of the known universe.

ASTRONOMY OF THE EASTERN WORLD

Some of the oldest records of observed lunar and solar eclipses come from China and date to the late Bronze Age, approximately one thousand years before the common era. The Chinese placed a unique and special emphasis on astronomical work, weaving it into the fabric of their imperial system. Chinese emperors expected their astronomers to provide extensive celestial calendars and give accurate predictions as to the recurrence of heavenly events. This expectation stems from the early Chinese belief that the emperor was thought to be a "son of heaven." As a result, the imperial leader's reputation was determined in part by the power of their astronomical achievements.

Chinese astronomers focused on observable patterns and used mathematics to calculate models for the movement of individual bodies. Where the Greeks were more concerned with extensive theories about the cosmos, the Chinese made great strides in the predictive functions of astronomy. They showed great interest in comets and other momentary events in the sky, each with its own opportunity to build a model to calculate the occurrence. Chinese astronomers recorded the observation of **sunspots** as early as 800 BCE; this predates the European "discovery" of sunspots by almost 2,000 years.

Astronomy in the Islamic world was enriched greatly by the work of Greek, Babylonian, and Indian astronomers. In the eighth century, Islamic astronomers began compiling charts and tables in order to plot the course of bodies in the solar system. These handbooks, known as *zij*, featured directions for finding and calculating movements using techniques gained primarily from Greek astronomy. The work of Ptolemy, an early Greek astronomer, was translated into Arabic and used as the basis of many innovations

A gnomon casts a shadow on a sundial, giving both time of day and astronomical information.

in planetary theory. The passage of time from Ptolemy's observations to the Islamic investigations offered a more comprehensive record of observed positions.

Later, in the thirteenth century, Islamic astronomers diverted more heavily from Ptolemy's work. They began to implement more mathematically complicated models that featured "epicycles." An **epicycle** is the movement of a small planetary body around the circumference of a larger planetary counterpart. This means that the small planet not only revolves around the larger one, but does so by traveling in circles around the circumference of its orbit.

In India, ancient astronomical traditions date back as early as the Indus Valley civilization, around 3000 BCE. Indian religions placed great importance on the constellations and associated celestial calendars. Texts on the proper performance of Indian religious rituals often included sections on mathematics and astronomy to ensure positional accuracy in the heavens. One of the earliest astronomical texts in the Indian repertoire dates back to about 700 BCE. The *Vedanga Jyotisha* featured a **lunisolar calendar**, which indicated both the moon phase and the time of the solar year, as well as observations on the sun and moon.

Later on, following the conquests of Alexander the Great in the fourth century BCE, Greek astronomical ideas began to cross-pollinate with Indian thought. The Indian tradition used an instrument called a **gnomon** to make astronomical assertions. The gnomon was effectively the vertical piece of a sundial that casts a shadow. These instruments were used to great effect in suggesting a way to determine the direction of the **meridian**, or a longitudinal circle that passes through both poles of the Earth's surface. With the measurements of the shadow from at least three separate positions, Indian astronomers could calculate where an observer is heading in relation to the equator.

RENAISSANCE ASTRONOMY

In the period that most immediately preceded the astronomical work of the Herschels, astronomy changed radically. The Renaissance, a period of cultural awakening in Europe that lasted from the fourteenth through seventeenth centuries, finally saw the abandonment of Earth-centric models of planetary movement. In the year 1543, Nicolaus Copernicus published a monumental text for the field of astronomy. *De Revolutionibus Oorbium Coelestium* assembled a **heliocentric** account of the solar system through a series of hard mathematical proofs. Using geometric strategies known to the ancient Greeks, he postulated an entirely new system for the orbital mechanics of the heavens. This spurred the so-called "Copernican Revolution" in astronomy, in which astronomers began to explore the fact that the sun—and not Earth—stood at the center of our solar system. Copernicus died in the very same year of his epic publication, leaving the scientific world to pick up where he had left off.

The brilliant hands of Galileo Galilei then took up the reins. This Italian astronomer, mathematician, and engineer argued throughout his career for the validity of the Copernican model. Galileo performed the first observation of the moons of Jupiter. In order to see these bodies in orbit, he had to construct a telescope that magnified the light from celestial bodies in the sky. Using a glass lens as the **refractor** in a telescope of his design and construction, Galileo successfully magnified the incoming light of the heavens by a factor of twenty with this new instrument. This engineering feat changed the course of astronomy yet again, as it meant the transition away from observations with the naked eye.

Galileo's impact on astronomy is evident from the ubiquity of telescopes as an astronomical instrument in the centuries that followed. His contributions range from the in-depth exploration of sunspots, to the empirical evidence that proved the existence of a heliocentric system. The latter contribution was met with serious opposition from both religious and scientific communities alike. Staunch defenders of Earth's central position in the solar system claimed that the heliocentric model was flawed because they believed it would necessitate a stellar **parallax**, or an evident shift in the position of stars, due to the ever-changing position of Earth around the sun. The absence of this parallax, to his critics, meant that Earth had to be a stationary body at the center of the solar system. However, Copernicus, years earlier, had correctly asserted that the immense distance of other stars from Earth would make the shift in parallax so small as to be imperceptible to the naked eye.

The Catholic Church also took serious issue with Galileo's claims. Given that numerous passages in the Bible appear to affirm Earth as the center of the universe, religious officials took heliocentrism to be a slight against their sacred text. As a result, Galileo was labeled as a heretic by the Pope himself, who demanded that he "[a]bandon completely ... the opinion that the sun stands still at the center of the world and the earth moves, and henceforth not to hold, teach, or defend it in any way whatever, either orally or in writing." The church eventually put him under house arrest, where he lived out his final years. In spite of this imprisonment, Galileo produced three more works of great scientific importance.

In many ways, Galileo blazed the trail for the work of Caroline and William Herschel as observational astronomers. The affirmation of a planetary framework proved integral to the advancement of astronomical work in the centuries that followed. With the improved understanding of Earth as a body in motion, more accurate models and calculations could be performed. The advent of the telescope as the primary astronomical instrument would allow for more accurate observations to be made of the night's sky. These two factors in tandem set the stage for the Herschels to dive right into astronomy as a field of new and profound opportunity.

ADVANCEMENTS IN OPTICS AND TELESCOPES

William's famous forty-foot telescope was truly a remarkable piece of equipment, allowing some of the first clear observations of distant nebulae in the universe. In order to build such an enormous instrument, William Herschel had to draw upon optical engineering practices proposed by astronomers and mathematicians in the century before. Nearly a hundred years earlier, the first reflector telescope began to take shape. Telescopes up until this point relied on the refraction of light through a glass lens to produce a magnified image in a tiny eyepiece. The magnification of this style of telescopes relied on the ratio of the lens's **focal length** to the focal length of the eyepiece. As a result, small eyepieces were desirable, making for a strained observational experience for astronomers.

The reflecting telescope, on the other hand, uses mirrors instead of lenses to focus light for the observer. Mirrors have a particular advantage over lenses in that they do not cause **chromatic aberration**. In a lens, chromatic aberration occurs when the refraction of light causes different colors in the spectrum of visible light to be more or less in focus. This happens due to the difference in wavelength between colors being refracted through the lens. In essence, these refracting telescopes could produce flawed images in which wavelength distortion masks the true characteristics of the observation.

Reflecting telescopes work by positioning a large **concave** mirror at the end of an open tube. As light enters the tube, it bounces off the mirror and focuses into a point based on the parabolic shape of the reflective surface. By calculating the focal point of this primary mirror, a secondary mirror can be placed to show the reflected light to an observer. There are a few configurations that can route the incoming light into the eyepiece. The first telescope of this kind was proposed by mathematician James Gregory in 1663. He published *Optima Promota*, which contained the layout for a reflecting telescope wherein the secondary mirror was positioned perpendicular to the focal point of the primary reflector. In order to get the light to the observer, the "Gregorian Reflector" required a small hole in the center of the primary mirror that allowed light to exit the tube.

Using Gregory's design as a model, Robert Hooke sought to create a prototype reflecting telescope. He quickly employed the services of a skilled instrument engineer and, within a year in 1664, had a working optical device. While the telescope succeeded as a working prototype, many practical constraints made its usage unreliable. For instance, the long tube that stretched out from the primary mirror had to be open at the end. This meant that dust and debris could easily accumulate on the reflector, producing faulty observations and requiring regular cleanings. Additionally, these

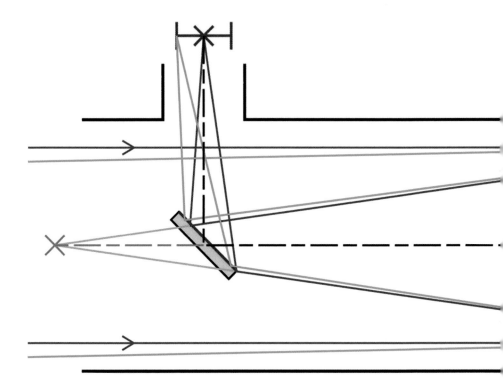

This diagram shows how light reacts with two reflectors in a Newtonian telescope.

early mirrors were made from copper and tin, which tarnished easily. Any loss of reflectivity would have to be remedied by an extensive polishing session. This required the removal of the primary reflector, meaning that the entire instrument would have to be recalibrated when it was reinserted.

In 1671, Isaac Newton had his own ideas for the reflective telescope. In his design, he proposed the position of a flat secondary mirror positioned at 45 degrees. This would make the light coming

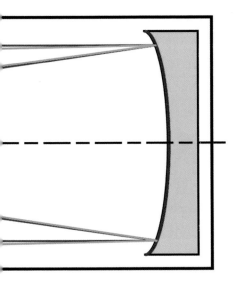

off of the primary mirror reflect at a right angle to an eyepiece in the side of the tube. This had the practical concerns of the astronomer in mind. By positioning the eyepiece closer to the center of the tube, observers could raise and lower the angle of the entire telescope without changing their sitting position.

A year later, French Catholic Priest and scholar Laurent Cassegrain made a significant innovation to the instrument. With Gregory's telescope in mind, Cassegrain implemented a **convex** mirror as a secondary reflector. The combination of a convex mirror in tandem with the concave primary reflector addressed a significant issue inherent to telescopes with two mirrors. While reflectors avoid distortions from chromatic aberration, the curvature of multiple reflectors causes a phenomenon common to both forms of optical magnification called "**spherical aberration.**" In an ideal **parabolic mirror**, all points of light are reflected perfectly to a single focal point. In reality, all mirrors contain slight imperfections, which result in spherical aberration. This distortion of light compounds when another reflector is added to an optical instrument.

The magnification of a reflective telescope is a function of the diameter of its primary mirror. The square of the primary mirror's diameter determines its optical capability. As an example, one could compare the light gathering power of two primary mirrors of forty- and eighty-inch diameters respectively. Because the light gathered by the reflector has a square relationship, the lens can produce images which would be four times fainter for a mirror half its size (40 × 40 = 1,600 and 80 × 80 = 6,400 thus 6,400/1,600 = 4). In terms of effective range of the reflectors, the eighty-inch mirror would be able to see objects which are twice as far away from Earth than its forty-inch counterpart.

It is easy to see how William Herschel developed the conviction that, when it came to primary reflectors, bigger was better. A larger primary mirror, however, required a much longer tube to place the focal point for the observer. The construction of a 40-foot focal length telescope was necessary to support the physical demands of a 49.5-inch diameter primary reflector. In contrast to his 20-foot reflecting telescope, which had a mirror of only 18.7" in diameter, the 40-foot monstrosity could gather light from sources well over twice the distance from Earth.

William Herschel did not simply take the design of other astronomers and scale it up, though. The Herschelian reflector innovated on the concept by removing the secondary reflector entirely. Instead, he positioned the primary reflector at an angle that bounced light directly to an observer at the focal point. Using this method, Herschel successfully avoided the problem of the tarnished reflective alloys used in secondary reflectors at the time. This meant that more time could be spent at the helm of the telescope without constant need for polishing and setup.

ASTRONOMICAL CURIOSITIES IN THE 1700S

Aside from the hard technological advances of optical instruments, astronomers in the eighteenth century were making strides towards answering both practical and theoretical scientific inquiries. Before the Herschels began celebrated careers as astronomers, scientists and mathematicians were hard at work with the best tools they had at their disposal. Early in the century, two English astronomers began to tackle a pressing question of the times: How does one most accurately determine a ship's longitude while at sea? Due to ever-changing weather conditions and constant movement on a boat, watches during this period could not stay accurate long enough to give sailors an indication of their longitude.

Reverends Humfrey Ditton and William Whiston set out to find a solution, which would have significant ramifications for travelers, merchants, and naval vessels alike. They first proposed a method by which ships could determine their position through a series of timely signals. In order to achieve this, ships would have to be positioned at regular intervals across primary oceanic routes. At the stroke of midnight, these ships would be expected to fire off a shell over a mile high. The pair of mathematicians calculated that a flare at that height could be observed both visually and audibly from a distance of eighty-five miles. When ships along the route saw the shell, they could make proper corrections to the time and alter their headings accordingly.

This solution, however clever, proved to be one of many at the time that never gained traction in British parliament. Every project in the category lacked practicality and ease of implementation. One such project suggested that sailors keep time by observing the movements of Jupiter's moons in the night sky. But operating a telescope large enough to make such a powerful observation would be very difficult on a ship that moved heavily in the tide. Alternatively, other astronomers tried to suggest the usage of lunar position to calculate time and longitude. This attempt could only provide ships with an accuracy of two or three degrees, unfortunately falling short of the requirement to achieve an allowance of a single degree of variance.

THE THREE BODY PROBLEM

Newtonian physics had given the eighteenth century a profound framework for the explanation of gravitational forces. His theories gave a comprehensive account for the movement of two bodies in relation to one another, but fell short in providing a theory for more complex models like that of the entire solar system. Astronomers of the time called this the **"three body problem"** in a quest to flesh out Newton's explanation for the forces of gravity present in systems where more than two bodies were in orbit. This problem required that astronomers take a set of data on three orbital bodies and use it to accurately and precisely calculate the future movements of all three. In the 1700s Earth, the moon, and the sun would be used as the subjects of experiments and calculations. As outlined in the previous section, academics at the time believed that proper understanding of lunar movements could lead to serious advancement in the search for longitudinal measurements at sea.

Jean Le Rond D'Alembert and Alexis-Claude Clairaut both made claims to the approximate solutions of the three-body problem. As rivals in the astronomical field, they both submitted their findings to the French Royal Academy of Science in the year 1747. Their "solutions" relied upon fundamental approximation and generality, however, and failed to produce absolute certainty about the movements of all three bodies at once. Over a hundred years later, mathematicians would go on to show that the problem produced an infinite number of possible solutions, revealing that the movements in a three-body system do not usually repeat with the exception of a few cases.

THE TRANSIT OF VENUS

Another popular project for astronomers during this period was to find ways to calculate the true distance of Earth from the sun. Some astronomers believed that this distance could be used as a standard measurement to express the distance of any body in the solar system. It was proposed that one way to calculate this distance was by observing the movement of Venus's orbit across the surface of the sun from Earth's perspective. If astronomers positioned at one area on the globe recorded the time it took for this **transit of Venus** to move completely from one edge of the sun to another, they could compare the time of their observation with other astronomers in different locations. This is called measuring the parallax, or difference, in perceived position in an object at two different vantage points.

This hypothesis looked promising for eighteenth century astronomers due to their understanding of basic trigonometry. Since the position of Venus during a solar eclipse placed the planet, by definition, directly in between Earth and the sun, astronomers used multiple vantage points to create a triangular relationship for the observation. If the distance between two observers was known, it could be used to create an isosceles triangle with Venus as the most acute vertex. By dividing the distance between astronomers, and consequently, the triangle in half, a right triangle is revealed. Since the difference of the observations in time can be expressed as a value in degrees, astronomers could use trigonometry and the Pythagorean theorem to calculate the

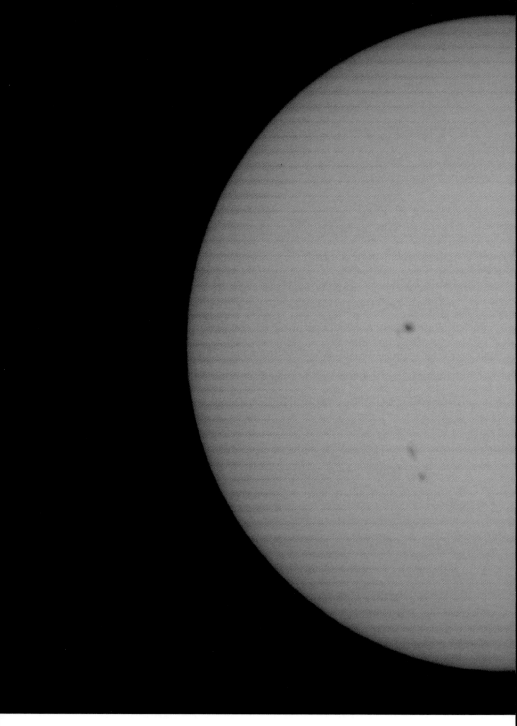

The rare transit of Venus across the surface of the sun as viewed from Earth

distance between Earth and Venus. With this information in hand, the astronomers could then calculate the distance between Earth and the sun.

Astronomers and mathematicians from a range of different countries set out in 1761 and 1769 to gather data on the transit of Venus. This event was hugely important to observe, as since then it has only occurred a total of four more times. Observations performed in North America in 1769 resulted in the calculation of a new, most-accurate measurement for the distance of Earth from the sun. At a distance of 24,000 times the radius of Earth, this measurement got within 3 percent of the current known distance of 92.96 million miles.

This profound event also produced the first hypothesis that Venus contained an atmosphere. Russian astronomer Mikhail Lomonosov observed an arc of light (later known as a Lomonosov arc) from the planet as it exited the transit across the sun. He claimed that this event was caused by the refraction of the sun's rays through a hazy atmosphere. His hypothesis would be confirmed with absolute certainty later. In modern times, astronomers recreated his experiment with a period-accurate refracting telescope for the 2004 transit of Venus. In an attempt to discount the initial hypothesis on the basis of inaccurate optical instruments, the researchers found much to their surprise that an exact replica of his experiment produced the same result.

WHAT FRUIT DOES THE EARTH MOST RESEMBLE?

Astronomy during this time was also greatly concerned with the nature and shape of Earth itself. Previous theories had tried to understand Earth as a spherical object not unlike an orange. Newton, on the other

NIGHTLY SWEEPS

During a period when so much astronomical work was being performed for the sake of theory, Caroline Herschel had a different goal in mind. Her focus on purely observational astronomy proved tremendously useful for centuries to come. She dedicated her working life to her sweeps of the heavens, documenting everything that she possibly could. One entry from her journal reads:

> "1795. May 1st.—In the future when any great chasms appear in my journals, it may be understood that sweeping for comets has not been neglected at every opportunity which did offer itself. But as I always do sweep according to the precept my brother has given me, and as I often am in want of time, I think it is very immaterial if the places where I have seen nothing are noted down."

She makes sure to note that any lack of entries in her journal is surely not from lack of observation. Her dedication to nightly sweeps (weather permitting) resulted in the massive catalogues of stars and nebulae we have today. Her biggest contribution to astronomy is surely her unconquerable passion for observation and discovery. While she, yet again, reverts to the modest admission that she's merely following William's orders, her quest is most definitely her own. This tireless but useful documentation is what produced a record-breaking number of comet discoveries.

hand, believed that the poles of the planet were flattened at both ends. As a result, he thought the planet was much more closely approximated by the form a grapefruit. Italian astronomer Giovanni Cassini thought just the opposite, that the poles would protrude slightly from the top and the bottom of the planet, much more like a lemon.

The year 1735 marked the first empirical investigation of claims regarding the shape of the planet. Even for a large expedition, this was a huge undertaking, requiring a decade of exploration to provide any kind of useful data. The French Academy of Science sent two groups to Earth's equatorial and polar regions. The expeditions to Peru and the arctic of Finland were expected to reveal important facts about the shape

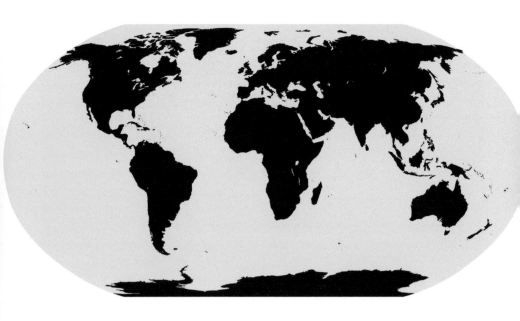

An image depicting the shape of the Earth as proposed by Sir Isaac Newton

of Earth based on its positional measurements. In order to perform these calculations, the groups took down the standard measurement of distance across an arc of one degree on Earth. The Peruvian arc measured a whole 2,334 feet (711 meteres) greater than the Finnish arc, proving a relative flatness at the poles, lending credence to Newton's grapefruit-shaped hypothesis.

While this test could hardly be considered comprehensive as to the shape of the entire Earth, it provided scientists in the eighteenth century with a bit of empirical evidence about the measurements of degrees on the surface of the planet. Modern science would later prove all three fruit theories incorrect with the advent of satellite imaging. Using data compiled by the work of many satellites, scientists have recently revealed the shape of Earth as an unshapely rock that appears spherical due to water coverage. In the classical sense of the investigation, science has revealed that Earth in fact most resembles a potato in shape.

Scottish science writer and astronomer Mary Somerville.

CHAPTER FOUR

CONTEMPORARIES, CRITICISMS, AND CONTROVERSIES

During the eighteenth and nineteenth centuries, Caroline Herschel was hardly the only female astronomer around. While she made history by becoming the first paid woman in science as well the first woman to submit a paper to the Royal Society, her contemporaries across the globe were also making profound discoveries. This chapter will give a glimpse into the lives of three other female astronomers during this time period. In many ways, these three women faced many of the same challenges as Herschel, having to work tirelessly to find a place in a male-dominated field. Additionally, their work shows a great range of contributions to the field, from observational discoveries to predictive calculations and astronomical models.

MARY SOMERVILLE

Mary Somerville, like Herschel, worked as an astronomer during the eighteenth and nineteenth centuries. Somerville bears a particularly significant link to Herschel in that she was also granted honorary membership to the Royal Astronomical Society at the same time. Born in Jedburgh, Scotland, in the year 1780, she was the daughter of a housewife and a Navy admiral. Her father, Admiral Sir William George Fairfax spent much time away serving out at sea. This left the young Somerville alone with her mother, who placed very little restriction on her daughter's upbringing aside from regular bible study and other religious obligations. This fact alone set her opportunities for self-discovery at a higher level than the young Herschel, unbound by constant expectations of household toil and labor.

In spite of fewer restrictions, Somerville's formal education was also lacking compared to the schooling allotted to men at the time. She attended an all girls' boarding school for a single year, receiving her first arithmetical lessons at age thirteen. This left her wanting more from an education in math, catching only a glimpse of basic math and its implementation. At the same time, however, the teenage Somerville found herself enrolled in a writing course where she read a range of different texts. One day, while perusing a magazine on women's fashion, she came across a puzzle section that piqued her interest. These puzzles contained challenges with algebraic equations and led her to seek more information on their solutions. Rather ironically, Somerville found a way to fill the gaps in her mathematical education by looking through a text for women during this time period. In a way, she used the best informal resources around her to make up for biases against educating women during this time. This prompted her to push her brothers to scrounge up any books or papers that they could so she could continue her quest in self-education.

Later in 1804, Somerville married a captain in the Russian naval force. Her husband, Samuel Greig, showed no interest in his bride's scientific or mathematical curiosities. During the three short years of their marriage, the newlyweds had two children. One of these children would go on to become a scientist himself from Somerville's teachings. The marriage was cut short by Greig's untimely death, leaving Somerville with a significant inheritance. This meant that she could pursue her intellectual curiosities at home without limitation, making the transition into the scientist she would soon become. She was met with the disapproval of friends and family alike for pursuing an interest in science as a woman. In spite of this constant criticism, Somerville spent years mastering contemporary physics and astronomy by studying the work of fellow Scottish astronomer James Ferguson and the famous Isaac Newton. In her personal recollections, Somerville writes:

> **❝** *I had studied plane and spherical trigonometry, conic sections, and Ferguson's* Astronomy. *I think it was immediately after my return to Scotland that I attempted to read Newton's Principia. I found it extremely difficult, and certainly did not understand it till I returned to it some time after, when I studied that wonderful work with great assiduity, and wrote numerous notes and observations on it.* **❞**

During this period of intense study, she married a man named Dr. William Somerville. Her new husband wholeheartedly endorsed her academic interests and pursuits. Armed with the education she worked tirelessly to attain, Somerville began her own scientific experiments on magnetism and solar rays in the year 1825. Second only to Herschel's paper on the discovery of her first comet, Somerville submitted the second-ever academic paper written by a female scientist to the Royal Astronomical Society. Entitled "The Magnetic Properties of the Violet Rays of the Solar Spectrum," this paper garnered respect immediately from the astronomical community. She would earn a reputation as a wonderfully talented scientific writer, publishing significant texts for the advancement of the entire scientific field.

Apart from personal investigations, Somerville gained much attention and respect for her translations of *Mécanique Céleste* (translated as *Celestial Motions*) by Pierre-Simon Laplace, resulting in the addition of her portrait bust into the Royal Astronomical Society's Great Hall. Laplace himself would go on to say famously to Somerville: "There have been only three women who have understood me. These are yourself, Mrs. Somerville, Caroline Herschel and a Mrs. Greig of whom I know nothing." Of course, "Mrs. Somerville" and "Mrs. Greig" were the same person.

Her own scientific achievements would stand the test of time as she went on to publish three major works in the field of physics and astronomy. In fact, her 1848 publication *Physical Geography* was taught as a textbook in formal academic classrooms for over fifty years. Her work also helped bring more popular attention to the brilliant work of Newton's *Principia Mathematica* through her published works and experiments. For her efforts, Somerville, much like Herschel, was granted a suitable salary as a scientific writer. This was only the second instance of a salary for a female scientist given by a governing body, setting a new precedent in a field previously dominated solely by men.

Somerville's contributions to science were very well regarded in her time. Upon her death, the London Post proclaimed her to be "The Queen of Nineteenth Century Science."

NICOLE-REINE LEPAUTE

Nicole-Reine Lepaute was an eighteenth-century mathematician and astronomer born in Paris, France, in 1723. Born twenty-seven years before Herschel, Lepaute made the majority of her discoveries before Herschel even picked up her first Newtonian sweeper. Lepaute is known for creating incredibly accurate astronomical clocks and calculating the occurrence of celestial events. Her husband, Jean-André Lepaute, worked as a royal clockmaker. Her husband's career allowed Mrs. Lepaute to persuade him to construct an astronomical clock, which she helped to engineer and build. Most famously, she worked with colleagues Alexis Clairault and Jerome Lalande to predict the return of Halley's Comet in 1759. While the trio miscalculated the comet's return by exactly a month's time, the models they used showed impressive understanding of the gravitational forces exerted by both Jupiter and Saturn upon the comet's path.

Lepaute's work, however, would not be recognized appropriately during her lifetime, due to the understatement of her contributions to the project. Both Clairault and Lalande published papers on their mathematical calculations but without proper mention of Lepaute's part in the discovery. Clairault snubbed her work completely with

A portrait of French astronomer and scholar Nicole-Reine Lepaute

the omission of her name from his article. Lalande made mention of her addition to the study but made no attempt to have her coauthor the paper. Lepaute, in spite of publishing articles under her own name in an astronomical magazine, was systematically denied the fame allotted to male astronomers of the same period. Such challenges seemed to improve only incrementally over the next century as Herschel and Somerville made unchallengeable claims to the scientific community. In one such article, Lepaute exactly predicted the arrival of a solar eclipse on April 1, 1764. The article included the correct fifteen-minute viewing periods across Europe as the eclipse cast a shadow across the continent.

Additionally, Lepaute worked with Lalande on providing calculations for the expected time and date of Venus's transit across the surface of the sun. The transit of Venus is similar to a solar eclipse, but the planet's size and distance from Earth makes it seem no larger than a travelling speck on the sun. After this contribution, Lepaute was named an honorary member of the Scientific Academy of Béziers.

WANG ZHENYI

Around this time, to the east in China, another female astronomer was making subversive contributions to the study of the heavens. Born in the Nanjing province of China in 1768, Zhenyi grew up as an avid reader with a sharp mind. Despite living in eighteenth-century China, she had a profound and self-directed education in the fields of astronomy, poetry, medicine, and mathematics. Her grandfather became her first mentor in astronomy with a large collection of over seventy books in his library. At the age of eighteen, she found the company of other female academics and became well known for her achievements across her many fields of study.

Zhenyi began at a very young age making significant contributions to science and mathematics. In a paper entitled "Dispute of the Procession of the Equinoxes," she provided, very plainly and simply, a way to calculate the movement of equinoxes in the sky. She also explored the subject of lunar eclipses by creating experiments using sunlight and a round mirror to represent the moon. By moving the "moon's" position around relative to a round table, which represented Earth, Zhenyi postulated mathematical relationships between the three objects at play. By publishing a paper titled "The Explanation of a Solar Eclipse," she continued to be a force for astronomy in China against all expectations of women. In fact, she would go on to teach her findings to male students, showing her skill as an educator and a figure of academic success. Zhenyi is quoted famously as saying that men and women "are all people, who have the same reason for studying." Perhaps most impressively, Zhenyi made all of these advances across many fields in her short life of only twenty-nine years.

THE RECEPTION OF HERSCHEL'S CONTRIBUTIONS TO ASTRONOMY

Herschel's letters and publications to the Royal Society show her monumental courage and diligence to participate in the scientific process of peer review. Peer review is a scientific practice in which other scientists in your field must study your work to determine if it meets acceptable standards. In observational astronomy, confirmation of discoveries by other astronomers becomes nearly equally important to the initial discovery itself in order to confirm the existence of a new celestial body. Across all fields of science, recreating results in the form of peer review is integral to the process of verification for a discovery. As a result, it is important to look at the way groups of her fellow astronomers looked upon her work following her discoveries.

As Herschel's first letter to the society showed, she approached the peer review stage with the utmost care and apology. Using the friendships of her brother, Herschel submitted her letter with great haste to the society, affording them the proper time window to observe her discovery with their own eyes. Members of the society then compared, with their own more complex optical instruments, the coordinates of Herschel's comet to the position of known bodies in the sky. After confirming her results, one of William's friends in the society responded to share the joy elicited by her humble observation. Alex Aubert wrote:

> *Dear Miss Herschel,—*
>
> *I am sure you have a better opinion of me than to think I have been ungrateful for your very, very kind letter of the 2nd August. You will have judged I wished to give you some account of your comet before I answered it. I wish you joy, most sincerely, on the discovery. I am more pleased than you can well conceive that you have made it, and I think I see your wonderfully clever and wonderfully amiable brother, upon the news of it, shed a tear of joy. You have immortalized your name, and you deserve such a reward from the Being who has ordered all these things*

to move as we find them, for your assiduity in the business of astronomy, and for your love for so celebrated and so deserving a brother. I have received your very kind letter about the comet on the 3rd, but have not been able to observe it till Saturday, the 5th, owing to cloudy weather. I found it immediately by your directions; it is very curious, and in every respect as you describe it.

"

Aubert's experiment proved Herschel's discovery to the society, making history with the tracking of her first comet. His letter begins with the niceties to be expected of a letter to a friend's sister. The tone of the letter strikes chords of admiration and wonder as Aubert claimed to celebrate the discovery with none other than Herschel's brother William. It is perhaps this proximity to the favorable reputation of William that lent Herschel such a warm reception from the society. This would continue to prove a boon for Herschel's contributions as future letters were met with the very same excitement.

This correspondence shows no hint of the devaluation of her work. Instead, later in the letter, Aubert gets directly to the matter at hand, sharing his micrometer measurements and remarking the precision of his tool. It was, no doubt, an impressive feat for Herschel to have made her discoveries on a telescope of such simple construction. In spite of its relative inaccuracy, Herschel's telescope provided the Society with all the information they needed to perform the same sweep and see the comet with their very own eyes.

As Herschel's comet discoveries increased, so too did admiration for her amongst the members of the Royal Astronomical Society. Eventually, Herschel would discover not just one, but eight comets—all of which would be confirmed by the society. After a number of her sweeping discoveries, Aubert continued to praise Herschel with an undying admiration for her efforts. One such letter from Aubert following the sighting of yet another comet reads:

> *You cannot, my dear Miss Herschel, judge of the pleasure I feel when your reputation and fame increase; everyone must admire your and your brother's knowledge, industry, and behaviour. God grant you many years health and happiness. I will soon pay you a visit, as soon as your brother returns. If I have any instrument you wish to use, it is at your service.*

Aubert, here, was absolutely right. Herschel became a bit of a local celebrity in her own right in both England and Hanover. Back home, the Herschel siblings were widely regarded for their academic endeavors. Caroline gained the respect of many astronomers and academics traveling through their observatories over the years. Nearly all of them spoke positively of her talents in astronomy. In a time period where comet discovery was the topic of many a high-class discussion, Herschel's name undoubtedly became the talk of the town.

In perhaps the most important response to her entire body of work, a letter penned by J. South, Esquire, to the Royal Astronomical Society outlines the case for awarding her the

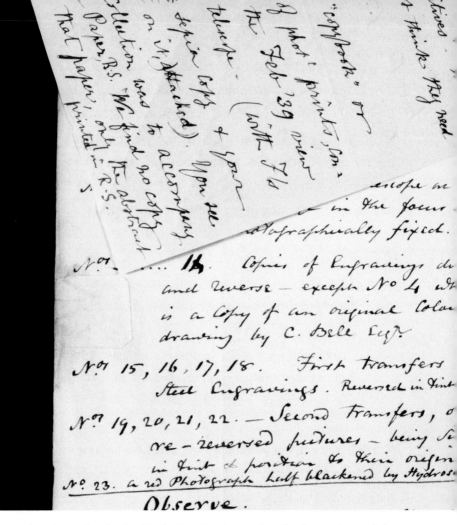

Pages from journals submitted to the Royal Society explore the discoveries made by the Herschel family.

Society's Gold Medal, the highest honor granted by the society. After explaining her contributions as a faithful assistant to William's famous sweeps, South writes:

> Her claims to our gratitude end not here; as an original observer she demands, and I am sure she has,

Caroline Herschel: Astronomer and Cataloger of the Sky

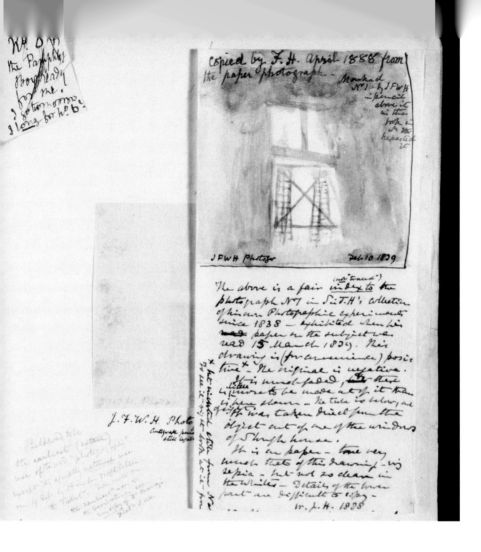

our unfeigned thanks. Occasionally her immediate attendance during the observations could be dispensed with. Did she pass the night in repose? No such thing: wherever her brother was, there you were sure to find her. A sweeper planted on the lawn became her object of amusement; but her amusements were of the higher order, and to them we stand indebted for the discovery of the comet of 1786, of the comet of 1788, *of the comet of 1791, of the comet of 1793, and of the comet of 1795, since rendered familiar to us by the remarkable discovery of [the comet] Encke. Many also of the nebulae contained in Sir W. Herschel's catalogues were detected by her during these hours of enjoyment. Indeed, in looking at the joint labours of these extraordinary personages, we scarcely know whether most to admire the intellectual power of the brother, or the unconquerable industry of the sister.* **”**

It was not just Herschel's discovery of comets, however, that garnered favorable review from the Royal Society. In fact, the Royal Society praised her primarily for her contributions to astronomy long after her days as an observer had passed. After William's death in 1822, Caroline took it upon herself to assemble massive collections of observations into condensed texts for the Royal Society's publication. In a book titled *The Reduction and Arrangement in the Form of a Catalogue, in Zones, of all the Star-Clusters and Nebulae Observed by Sir W. Herschel in his Sweeps*, she compiled all of the data from decades of observation with William's famous telescopes. This book was described by Sir David Brewster as "a work of immense labour," and "an extraordinary monument to the unextinguished ardour of a lady of seventy-five in the cause of abstract science." The Royal Society hailed Herschel by awarding her with the Gold Medal for this achievement. South's address to the society continues:

> **«** *In the year 1797 she presented to the Royal Society a Catalogue of 560 stars taken from Flamsteed's observations, and not inserted in the British Catalogue, together with a collection of errata that should be noticed in the same volume.*
>
> *Shortly after the death of her brother, Miss Herschel returned to Hanover. Unwilling, however, to relinquish her astronomical labours whilst anything useful presented itself, she undertook and completed the laborious reduction of the places of 2,500 nebulae, to the 1st of January, 1800, presenting in one view the results of all Sir William Herschel's observations on those bodies, thus bringing to a close half a century spent in astronomical labour.* **»**

The Royal Society chose to award Herschel their most prestigious award, not for her work as an assistant, but for the immense contributions she made to astronomy of her own accord. They recognized the indomitable passion of a woman who used the fortunes of a long life to continue making strides in her studies. Long after many retire in their careers, Herschel still showed a remarkable passion for astronomy, taking it upon herself to continue publishing works of importance for the field.

CRITICISM THROUGH SOCIAL POSITION

Criticism of Herschel's work was somewhat rare due to the respect she garnered in the field. Direct criticism by professionals is hardly, however, the only way in which her place on the scientific stage could

SATIRICAL CRITICS OF HERSCHEL'S WORK

While the work of Herschel was famously well received by the Royal Astronomical Society, her position as a female astronomer and comet hunter came under fire from popular satirists of the time. The illustrator R. Hawkins drew a comic showing a vulgar image of Herschel behind the telescope observing a "comet." The speech bubble above her head read, "What a strong sulphurous scent proceeds from this meteor." While the image amounts to nothing more than a lowbrow fart joke lampooning the accomplishments of a serious astronomer, the speech bubble implies something far more insulting. Hawkins seems to suggest that the "female philosopher" knows not the difference between a meteor and a comet, remarking upon the oddity of a sulphurous trail. This criticism is unsurprisingly baseless and indicative of the general misogyny toward female academics common to eighteenth and nineteenth century Britain.

Another comic taking Herschel for its subject commented on the presumed obsession with comet discovery during this time period. Since Herschel largely contributed to the increased public interest in the discovery of comets, this critique stands to question the value of her diligent astronomical work. Three unnamed figures are included in the comic, and the inclusion of a female figure appears to take jabs at the social dynamics of society. The interest of the woman and her fawning companion show a kind of naivety for the process of comet hunting and its perceived importance.

A satirical comic takes aim at society's increased interest in comet hunting.

be questioned. In a more important sense, the patriarchal society in which her work came about stood to devalue her accomplishments as a woman and as a scientist. Specifically, the formal structures of academic science ruled by men denied her the very title of scientist. In her lifetime, Herschel was known both on paper and in public opinion to be an astronomer's assistant and not an astronomer in her own right.

This fact stemmed undoubtedly from the inauguration of her position as the first woman to be paid a salary for scientific work. The king had Herschel listed as an assistant to William in the budget. While this position was unprecedented at the time, it did falsely promote the perception that any and all work she performed was at the behest of her brother's orders. This view of her and her work continued long after her death in spite of her many accomplishments and papers written entirely in William's absence. In fact, even today in the twenty-first century, there are historians and biographers who refuse to call Herschel a scientist. They opt instead to emphasize her role as a servant to the astronomical process.

Michael Hoskin, a well-known contemporary biographer of the Herschels, asserts that Caroline acted only in accordance to her brother's wishes without a semblance of original thought for the process. While the details of her life and avid explorations of the heavens stand in stark contrast to such an assertion, Hoskin's claim is hardly an isolated incident. In the biography entitled *Caroline Herschel, Priestess of the New Heavens*, Hoskin boldly states:

> ❝ *Although her discovery of comets brought her welcome fame, in her own right and not as an assistant to her brother, she had no interest in comets as such. There*

is no hint that she ever wondered about the physical makeup of the comets she had discovered, or their role in the economy of nature (to refuel the Sun, perhaps), or even whether they would return. She was, in short, no scientist. She was an obedient gundog, told to go and retrieve trophies. William had equipped her with the tools she needed and sent her out into the night with instructions to come back with comets, and this she had done, no fewer than eight times. As a result she was feted among male astronomers and famous among the general public, and understandably this gave great pleasure to the sometime scullery-maid. But the history of astronomy would have been much the same if she had never found a comet. As an observer, her great contribution had been to demonstrate to William, back in 1783, that nebulae in great numbers were awaiting discovery. 〞

It is curious how anyone in such great contact with the facts of her life could insist that she had no claim to the title of scientist and astronomer. Hoskin appears to be making the strange assertion that Herschel, in focusing on the purely observational aspects of astronomy, denies herself the right to be called a "real" scientist. When the time period is taken into account, it becomes obvious how her contributions and discoveries played an integral role in the advancement of astronomy as a field. In the eighteenth and nineteenth centuries, astronomical projects and hypotheses were usually radical and outlandish, clinging only to the astronomical framework provided by Newtonian physics and other recent advancements. The true "work" being done at the time was surely the measurements and calculations of celestial bodies in relation to one another. In other words, it matters not that men at the time thought that comets could be meant to "refuel the sun, perhaps." The scientific work that stood the test of time proved, instead, to be purely observational in nature.

Herschel's tireless work to create a comprehensive inventory of the night's sky went on to inspire profound scientific work in generations to come Hoskin was wrong to say that "the history of astronomy would have been much the same if she had never found a comet." It is incredibly significant that not only were these comets discovered, but that they were discovered and written about by a woman in eighteenth-century Britain. Astronomy would not be the same if the history books read that yet another male astronomer performed her observations. The time period in which she made her observations was critically important for the next round of British astronomers. In fact, William's son, John Herschel, became a notable astronomer building upon Caroline's later works, which compiled and systematized numerous decades of observations and calculations.

Even today, contemporary perceptions of Caroline Herschel's contributions belittle her important work. Some museums still do not list Herschel as an astronomer in her own right. The Smithsonian National Air and Space Museum features a small section on the Herschel siblings and their contributions to astronomy. The caption below their portraits reads "William Herschel: The Complete Astronomer" and then "Caroline Herschel: William's Essential Assistant." Again, the work and accomplishments of Herschel are devalued by her demotion from astronomer to "essential assistant."

The way in which the facts about her life are remembered shows that historians still have a number of hurdles to overcome in giving proper credit to the work of women in science. While Herschel called herself an assistant at times, this was a result of the society in which she lived. Contemporary science certainly should liberate Herschel from her position as a mere assistant in order to more accurately depict her contributions as a scientist.

Aug.ᵗ 1.ˢᵗ 1786.   C.H.ˢ 1.ˢᵗ Comet

I saw the object in the center of fig
...ke a star out of focus
...hile the others were
...rfectly clear. the
...rec. star is very faint
...t the weather is
...azy, and in a clearer
...ght undoubtedly some
...ore will be visible

They make now a
...erfect ...
...his figure is right

I

II

III

Caroline Herschel's first discovery
of a comet submitted to the Royal
Astronomical Society.

I think the situatio...
...is now like in fig
...but it is so hazy
...that I could only ima...
I saw the second star

CHAPTER FIVE

CAROLINE HERSCHEL'S IMPACT AND LEGACY

B y the end of her long, illustrious career as an astronomer, Herschel made a number of profound contributions to the field of observational astronomy. In addition to her academic successes, Herschel also blazed the trail for the future of women in science. Her discoveries are important for science due not only to their intrinsic merit, but because they signify the accomplishments of her individual work as a woman at the time. During a career spent mostly by the side of her distinguished brother, Herschel set herself apart when she took to the fields for observation alone with her modest telescope. It was in these moments of diligent solitude that Herschel laid claim to an unprecedented amount of discoveries. Over the course of eleven years, she documented the first sightings of eight comets. In spite of her occupation assisting William in large observational projects, Caroline took every clear night in her brother's absence to perform work of great astronomical importance.

HERSCHEL'S PERSONAL COLLECTION OF COMETS

On August 1, 1786, Herschel took her small Newtonian sweeper out into the field in spite of hazy conditions. In her methodical sweeps, she compared every observation with the known catalogs of the times. Some of the items in the astronomical inventory were even fresh additions made by William and Caroline in the preceding months and years. This meant that her observations were truly on the cutting edge of observational astronomy in the eighteenth century. With the catalog in hand, Herschel made an observation that could not be accounted for in any list. The hazy conditions produced a reasonable doubt within her observation, but the position was logged for further analysis. The following night, the clouds parted, giving definitive evidence for the first comet ever discovered by a woman of science.

With great haste and conviction, Herschel set out to report her findings to the Royal Astronomical Society. The unfortunate speed of postal services during this period meant that time was of the essence. Her letter arrived to members of the Society two weeks after the initial discovery of the comet. Astronomer Charles Messier, who was responsible for the most comprehensive catalog of the sky pre-Herschel, made a naked eye observation of her comet on August 17 of the same year. This meant that, using the document provided by some of the best astronomers of the time, Herschel beat those very astronomers to the discovery of a new comet in her personal observations. This comet, under the contemporary naming conventions, bears the title "C/1786 P1 Herschel." And so the first comet in history went down in the books named after the woman who discovered it.

Two years later, Herschel found herself before another undocumented celestial body. On December 21, 1788, she observed an object that was slightly brighter in the center with a non-uniform shape. This discovery would be tracked over the nights that followed, confirming the object was on the move. Herschel's documentation of positional data would provide astronomers at the Royal Society with enough to calculate a parabolic orbit. This new comet would be tracked over the course of an entire year. The immediacy of Herschel's discovery and documentation provided astronomers with a large window of time to take measurements and make calculations to hypothesize the path of the comet.

This discovery now has the name "Comet 35P/Herschel-Rigollet." This is because the comet was observed again a century and a half later by French astronomer Roger Rigollet. In 1939, Rigollet's observation was confirmed to be identical to Herschel's comet of 1788 from calculations performed by astronomer L.E. Cunningham. This comet will not be observable from Earth until the later half of the twenty-first century.

Early in the year 1790, Herschel continued her streak with yet another discovery of a comet. This observation was particularly timely and valuable because of the fleeting nature of the light from this comet. Only three days of observation provided Herschel with the information she needed to posit this third discovery. Messier, in his observations, noted the presence of a "nebulous" bright object. This note came, yet again, two weeks after Herschel's initial discovery and just two days before the comet's last observation in the eighteenth century sky. Herschel's name was yet again awarded to the discovery of this comet "C/1790 A1 (Herschel)."

With the passing of only three months, Herschel struck again with her fourth comet discovery. On April 18, 1790, Herschel observed a faint light without the discernible tail that is characteristic of comets. Over time, however, she tracked the object, which grew in brightness as its orbit brought it closer to Earth. The comet brightened by an order of three magnitudes, revealing at last a tail four degrees in length. She would track "Comet C/1790 H1" for two months until its disappearance in June of the same year.

Herschel's next discovery would be the first new comet observed by anyone on Earth since her last almost two years prior. In December of 1791, "Comet C/1791 X1 (Herschel)" was sighted for the first time with her Newtonian sweeper. Her description of the comet was a "pretty large, telescopic comet" which means that it was too faint to be seen with the naked eye. Her findings were yet again documented and reported to the society. The last glimpse of this comet was made by Messier on January 28 the following year. The short window of observation could be attributed to the growing distance of the comet from Earth along its orbit.

On October 7, 1793, Herschel made another observation of a bright comet in the sky. Without any record of the comet, she had no way of knowing that the comet had in fact been first discovered by Messier two weeks prior. This one, as a result, has the name "Comet C/1793 S2 (Messier)," to mark the comet's original observer. It is truly impressive how consistently Herschel made her astronomical observations with such modest tools during the same time frame as her famous male contemporaries. Herschel's constant observational vigilance put her at the forefront of astronomical discovery. This hard work and dedication alone turned her into the famed comet hunter we know her to be today.

January of 1786 brought the "Comet 2P/Encke" into view for astronomers. French observer Pierre Mechain noticed a bright object in the sky and quickly notified Messier of the potential comet. Astronomers worked over the next few days to try and catch glimpses of the observation without much luck. On January 19, the evening revealed the comet as it moved quickly across the sky. Just as quickly as it appeared, however, the comet eluded sight once again. This provided astronomers with only two observational data points, preventing the calculation of any orbit or path across the sky. Some ten years later, Herschel spotted this rare comet and was able to track it during a span of three weeks. From this new data, it was determined that the comet's path was not parabolic in nature, but more accurate calculations were not possible.

Twenty years after its initial discovery, the comet was observed once more. German astronomer Johann Encke took all the recorded observations and was able to put together a more comprehensive picture of an elliptical orbit. While his calculations for the period of 12.1 years were still incorrect, they got astronomers far closer to the actual movement of the comet. Precise measurements would not be recorded by Encke until 1818, when he mathematically proved that four decades of observations were of the same comet. The comet is named after Encke for his contributions in discovering the comet, all while relying on the work of Messier, Herschel, and other famous astronomers.

The eighth and final comet discovered by Herschel once again bears her name in the history books. This time, Herschel made her discovery almost simultaneously with astronomer Eugene Bouvard. Their records show the documented observation just hours apart on the same night. Thus, "Comet C/1797 P1 (Bouvard-Herschel)" has both their names attributed to the discovery. This comet was immensely bright and visible to the naked eye. Later records show that it may be the thirteenth-closest comet to Earth in its orbital path. As a result,

CAROLYN S. SHOEMAKER

Born June 24, 1929, Carolyn Shoemaker grew up in Gallup, New Mexico. Her career started as a seventh-grade teacher, which provided her with little inspiration. Shoemaker decided to leave teaching to start a family and married planetary scientist Gene Shoemaker in 1951. At the age of fifty-one, she began work as a field assistant to her husband following the departure of her fully grown children. This work involved the analysis of impact craters and geological surveys, which got her interested in both asteroids and comets. In the 1980s, her scientific career took off at Northern Arizona University where she began studying the movement of planet-crossing asteroids.

In 1992, she discovered "Comet Shoemaker-Levy 9" along with astronomer David H. Levy. This marked the first observation of an orbital collision in space as they observed the comet growing closer and closer as it orbited the planet Jupiter. In 1994, the comet made impact with the surface of Jupiter and broke into many illuminated fragments. This observation played a big role in astronomers' understanding in Jupiter's role in blocking debris in the middle of the solar system.

Shoemaker would continue to make discoveries using a combination of a wide-field telescope with a **stereoscope**. She used the stereoscope to identify objects in the sky against the backdrop of fixed stars. The stereoscope provides two different vantage points, which allow for approximated imagery in three dimensions. Shoemaker used this technique to reveal distant objects with high precision. Over twenty years of observations, Shoemaker discovered 32 new comets in addition to a number of asteroids totaling over 800. This shattered the record previously held by anyone and continued Herschel's legacy as a female comet hunter.

Carolyn Shoemaker in an observatory conducting astronomical research.

it moved with great haste across the sky between August 14 and 16, 1797, where it grew in brightness and intensity.

With eight comets in her observational portfolio, Herschel definitively set the record for discoveries by a woman. She made every discovery on her own with modest means and still managed to break astronomy records. Herschel's name would hold the coveted title of female comet hunter until two centuries later. In the 1980s another female astronomer would step into the limelight as the foremost comet seeker of all time.

Herschel's comet discovery record, while impressive, is far from her only contribution to the field of astronomy. In fact, while many of the comets are named after her, Herschel's most prestigious awards were granted for her many contributions to and publications for the Royal Astronomical Society. Of these many publications, one paved the way for astronomical study in both the immediate and foreseeable future. In 1786, William and Caroline compiled the findings of their sweeps into a central catalogue. This collection was called "The Catalogue of Nebulae and Clusters of Stars" and featured a comprehensive set of observations laid out in a methodical manner.

Herschel spent a good deal of time during the chaotic periods of their observations creating important texts for use by the Royal Society. Two publications stand out which are still referenced today as a powerful inventory of the night's sky from the northern hemisphere. The first is entitled "A Catalogue of 860 Stars Observed by Flamsteed, but not Included in the British Catalogue," in which Herschel diligently compiled information to be used by astronomers. This kind of consideration for the practical aspects of astronomy is integral to the practice as a whole. Without proper reference material,

The Gold Medal is awarded by the Royal Astronomical Society for an outstanding career in service to astronomy.

the act of making observations with large impressive telescopes would be both inefficient and burdensome. Herschel put in the tireless hours necessary for the advancement of all astronomers by improving the tools used in tandem with optical instruments.

She did not stop there, however, and presented the society with yet another collection of vital information for the field of astronomy. Within the span of ten years, she published this second compilation entitled "A General Index of Reference to Every Observation of Every Star in the Above-Mentioned British Catalogue." This text, paired with the previous one, provided astronomers with a powerful toolkit for discovery and study. With records of the collected observations in conjunction with information about positional relationships, Herschel all but eliminated the need for cross-referencing multiple volumes of astronomical information. With the data all in one place, she streamlined the observational process of the scientific method on the whole for astronomers.

After William's death in 1822, Herschel continued her efforts to package the immense amount of astronomical work they had performed as a duo. In a collection that went unpublished from the Royal Society, Herschel put many hours in her old age to the task of still more useful compilations. A text called "The Reduction and Arrangement in the Form of a Catalogue, in Zones, of all the Star-Clusters and Nebulae Observed by Sir W. Herschel in his Sweeps," provided an even more extensive framework for the practical usage of the siblings' astronomical findings. In this volume, she performed countless calculations to simplify and relate points of data together. Armed with decades of astronomical mathematics, Herschel took it upon herself to do the heavy lifting for future astronomers interested in testing their theories with the records of twenty- and forty-foot telescopic findings.

While the Royal Society never formally published this collection, it saw near immediate use in the advancement of astronomical theories. William Herschel, by this point, had since passed away, leaving behind a legacy of engineering and astronomical discoveries. In addition to his esteemed reputation, William made one last important contribution to the field of astronomy. He fathered a son, John Herschel, who would grow up to make profound discoveries of his own right in the same field. As a prodigal son of astronomy, John grew up around the expertise of his loving aunt who felt compelled to provide him with a top-notch education. Caroline began tutoring John at a young age and provided him with a number of important tools. Paramount among them was this final comprehensive collection of the Herschel observational legacy.

HERSCHEL AND HER NEPHEW JOHN

John Herschel was born in 1792 in the thick of his family's astronomical labors. Raised in Slough, where his father and aunt were performing observations of extremely distant objects, John was immediately in contact with the scientific and astronomical process. At a young age, his aunt exposed him to the wonders of Flamsteed's Almanac, giving him a rotund vocabulary of celestial bodies and events. Studies in astronomy, mathematics, chemistry, and botany brought the young John Herschel to Eton College and St. John's College in Cambridge. There, he made alliances with other men of profound intelligence. A friendship sparked between John and his colleague Charles Babbage, who would go on to engineer the first mechanical computer.

When he returned from his undergraduate career, John Herschel began working with his father and aunt in their astronomical efforts. Equipped with a sharp mind and important resources, he began to construct his own twenty-foot reflecting telescopes for personal observations. The young astronomer would quickly enjoy fame and the adoration of astronomers in the Royal Society. Two years before William's death, John would become one of the founding members of the reorganized Royal Astronomical Society in the form that remains to this day.

Caroline's condensation of decades of observations became immediately useful to John in his quest to continue the family profession.

Astronomer, mathematician, and chemist Sir John Herschel

John set out to reexamine the observations of double stars made by his father and aunt in attempts to make bolder mathematical claims about their relationships. Using the technological advancements made by the Herschel family, John set out to use powerful reflecting telescopes to record specific qualities in double star formations. This included color, size, brightness, and orbital path as a thorough investigation of the nature of stars in general.

With over 400 double star observations made and recorded by his family, John Herschel set out to add greatly to this collection for study. From 1821 to 1823, John began his own collection of double stars that documented 381 additions. Without the use of his aunt's immense volumes of information, the young Herschel would have had to perform an intense amount of work before even reaching the starting line of his observations. Instead, he was able to jump right into the astronomical game with a career that would quickly dwarf his father's in terms of observed double stars. From Caroline's diligent inventory system, John also learned to assemble information in a most efficient and useful manner. Astronomers needed only to follow the columns of the catalogue to learn about the properties of these double stars. This made it easy to see if an observation had been determined to be a mere **optical double** or an actual binary star system.

John Herschel was motivated largely by the task of proving his father's theories about the nature of double stars and the existence of binary solar systems. During regular correspondence with his beloved aunt, John mentioned that he had succeeded with this collection of 381 double stars in providing such evidence for William's double-star theory. An excerpt from one letter reads, "We have now verified not less than seventeen connected in **binary systems** in the way pointed out by my father, and twenty-eight at least in which no doubt of a material change having taken place can exist." This proved not only the value of his father's theories, but the value of the sheer observational efforts of William and Caroline in the late eighteenth century. Without that work as a foundation, it is hard to say that John would have so ravenously pursued the truth of this particular inquiry.

Using the tutelage of his father and aunt, along with the inventories of stars and nebulae, John Herschel began to venture into his own astronomical theories and observations with great conviction. The proof of double star systems provoked an entirely new field of astronomical study. John believed that this contribution, among many made by his father and aunt, was the most important of the century. Compared with the discovery of the planet Uranus, he claimed that it "was but a trifle compared to this, which I look upon as one of the greatest ever made by man." In addition to the importance of studying binary star systems, the identification of the optical doubles proved to be equally important to astronomical pursuits. Optical doubles could be used to great effect to determine parallax or observed positional change based on multiple vantage points. This meant that astronomers had even more tools at their disposal to measure the distance of various celestial bodies from one another based on trigonometric calculations.

With this set of identifications in hand, John Herschel set out to propose a new theory for the way in which astronomers use parallax to make measurements. Astronomers of the time believed that one had to measure the angular distance between the two stars of an optical double pair. Because these objects were so tremendously far away, John determined that instrumentation during this period was flat out incapable of making such a determination. He was right about that fact and decided to propose a new method for the use of parallax in astronomical measurements. Instead of using the angular distance of the two stars, John Herschel proposed the use of angular position of the stars, which could be determined relative to other known objects in the sky by his telescopes. He published a paper on the subject but worked only theoretically in outlining methods, instrumentation, and calculations for determining parallax without being the first astronomer himself to make such a measurement.

After an extended period of theoretical work, John Herschel would return to the same kind of work performed by his family before him. Interested less and less by the implications of the double stars, he set out to dramatically increase the size of the catalog by sweeping the sky. With a method practically synonymous with the Herschel name, John made an unprecedented amount of discoveries over the course of his career as an observer. By the year 1858, he had recorded a whopping total of 5,449 double stars of his own discovery. He published countless catalogs year after year of 300 or 400 double stars, steadily increasing the count as he went. By the end of his career, which spanned nearly a century, the total count of observed double stars in astronomy reached a count of over 10,000.

This career granted John the undying admiration of the Royal Society, which named him president on three different occasions. In 1826, he was awarded the Gold Medal of the Royal Astronomical Society for his many contributions. At the center of all his accomplishments, John relied upon the work of his family. In particular, after the passing of his father, Caroline provided her wisdom, guidance, and reference materials in complete and humble servitude to John's meteoric rise as an astronomer. Caroline's dedication to her nephew is evident in the many letters that they penned to one another. Many observations, theories, and musings were shared. All the while, his faithful aunt worked to provide him with the basis for a catalogue that is still used to this day. John Herschel published an updated version of the "General Catalogue of Nebulae and Clusters of Stars" in 1864. This collection would be later adapted by astronomers into the "New General Catalogue," which is still used by astronomers all over the world as a reference.

HERSCHEL'S INDUCTION TO THE ROYAL SOCIETY

The Herschel name was revered by all at the Royal Astronomical Society for the family's undying dedication to progress in celestial observation. John's fame and recognition, in particular, provoked deeper investigations into the family's contributions as a whole. This meant that Caroline's work was finally brought up for discussion to the society for the purpose of recognition. For the first time in history, the British scientific community sat down to look at the contributions of a woman in the field of astronomy. While it is unfortunate that it required her blood relation to two widely celebrated male astronomers, the Royal Society gave serious consideration to the prospect of hailing the work of a woman in science.

In the year 1828, Herschel was awarded the Royal Society's most prestigious honor of the Gold Medal for her work as an "assistant" to her brother William. This was the first time that the Gold Medal had been awarded to a woman and marked the undeniable right Herschel claimed to the field of astronomy. In perhaps a more astonishing honor, the society looked once again at her contributions seven years later. This

*This portrait of Caroline Herschel was commissioned for the
Royal Astronomical Society.*

time, the society looked not only at the tireless work she performed with William during sweeps, but at the record-breaking total of eight comet discoveries across her career. With the scope of her life's work clearly in view, the Royal Society made Herschel an honorary member in the year 1835.

The classification of "honorary member" as opposed to "member" shows a separation, still, between how Herschel's work was viewed in contrast to her male contemporaries. That being said, the designation was still completely unprecedented at the time. In fact, it would continue to be an anomaly for the Royal Society for over a hundred and fifty years after they bestowed the honor upon Herschel. In the year 1996, American astronomer Vera Rubin would break the 171-year streak of complete male domination in the Royal Astronomical Society with her induction for work on the rate of galaxy rotation.

HERSCHEL'S LEGACY AND THE AMERICAN FEMALE COMET HUNTER

However, Caroline Herschel's life and work had an influence that extended beyond the impressive accomplishments of her nephew. Perhaps more importantly, Herschel set a new precedent for the possibility of women in astronomical study. In her lifetime, her work would inspire another woman in the field of astronomy across the Atlantic Ocean. A few years prior to Herschel's reception of the Royal Society's Gold Medal, a woman by the name of Maria Mitchell was born in Nantucket, Massachusetts. Born into a family of Quakers in the year 1818, Mitchell was raised and educated alongside her nine brothers and sisters. Due to a Quaker belief about gender equality in education, she received a good foundation in reading and arithmetic from local schools. When she was eleven, her father

American astronomer and comet hunter Maria Mitchell works using her personal telescope.

began construction on a school of his own whereby Mitchell would be a student and teacher's aide.

Mitchell's astronomical education started from a very young age. Her father kept a telescope that was used to teach her about the heavens. With such a strong educational upbringing, Mitchell quickly took to pragmatically applying mathematics to astronomy. At the age of twelve, she successfully calculated the occurrence of an annular eclipse alongside her father. Her love of education and books would continue in a career of teaching at a Unitarian school. From here she transitioned into the job of librarian, which she kept for twenty years. The librarian position afforded her the opportunity to read and study. All the while, her father was working for the Pacific Bank as a cashier, which provided him with enough of a salary to indulge his astronomical curiosities. With his wage, William Mitchell constructed an observatory on the roof of his house. Using this, he made he made observations for the US Coast Guard.

With a telescopic observatory in place, Maria Mitchell had both the knowledge and the tools to make astronomical calculations and observations. One night, when assisting her father with observations for the coast guard, Mitchell came across an object that she determined to be a comet. Intrigued, she stationed herself behind the eyepiece of her father's telescope night after night to track the movements of the comet across the sky. After confirming through multiple nights of observation, William Mitchell reached out to an academic friend of his at Harvard University. In his letter, he proclaimed his daughter's discovery of a new comet. By this point, the only other woman to have discovered a comet was Caroline Herschel.

News spread quickly and America's first female comet hunter came into the limelight. Harvard professor William Bond took the news of Mitchell's discovery and relayed it to none other than the King of Denmark. Denmark's king, who was a self-proclaimed astronomical enthusiast, had a bounty out for the first discovery of a comet that could not be viewed with the naked eye. Mitchell had indeed made such a discovery of a telescopic comet and was promptly awarded a gold medal by the King. The comet would go down in history as "**Miss Mitchell's Comet,**" putting her name next to the illustrious Herschel.

Over the course of her astronomical career, Mitchell found herself in close contact with the Herschel family. During the 1850s, she made a trek across Europe visiting many sites of academic interest. She spent her time meeting with scientists and visiting observatories across multiple countries. In one such encounter, she met with John Herschel and his daughter Rose. They became friends instantly, sparking a relationship that would last the rest of Mitchell's life. John Herschel, knowing Mitchell's reputation as a comet hunter, bestowed upon her a great and meaningful gift: a page of Caroline Herschel's notebook.

This shows, truly, the strong connection between the work of Herschel and the profound importance it had on a female astronomer of the same century. Herschel's impact traveled through the loving mind of her nephew to reach a new generation of accomplished women in science. John's praise of his distinguished aunt stretched far and wide in the scientific community, inspiring many with the tales of her perseverance and dedication to astronomy. Mitchell, in particular, rose to the occasion of holding the torch passed by Herschel.

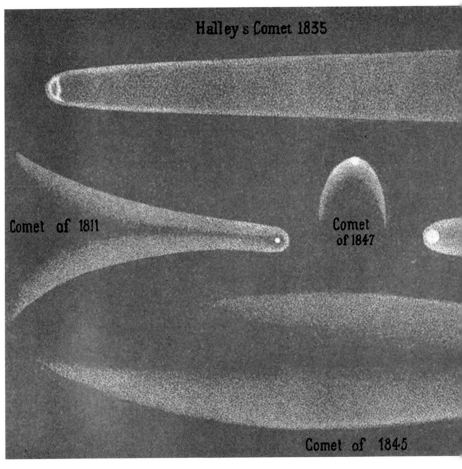

Halley's Comet 1835

Comet of 1811

Comet of 1847

Comet of 1845

These important comets were all discovered in the nineteenth century.

In the year 1865, Mitchell was appointed professor of astronomy at Vassar College. The observatory at Vassar had a telescope, which at the time was the third largest in the continental United States. From this vantage point, she would go on to make a number of important discoveries and calculations.

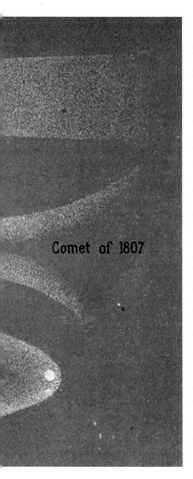

Comet of 1807

This was another tremendous milestone for women in science. Prior to this moment, no female astronomer had held a professorial position at any university. Looking with determination down the trail blazed by Herschel, Mitchell continued to strive for excellence in the field of astronomy. Herschel was the first woman to be granted a salary (however meager) for scientific work in the field of astronomy. Taking things a step further, Mitchell identified her value to the university in terms of her experience and contributions and determined that her salary needed to be renegotiated. She was awarded a raise and charged ahead with the power of new technological advances. Mitchell spent time not only observing stars but photographing them with cameras that were just being engineered.

For her extensive career and her contributions to astronomy, Mitchell was given yet another honor. In a similar fashion to Herschel, Mitchell became the first female member of the American Philosophical Society. She was elected as a full member for her distinguished career as an academic astronomer. Moreover, she used this position as a jumping off point to found the **American Association for the Advancement of Women**. Inspired by the work and legacy of Herschel, the first "professional" female astronomer in the same century, Mitchell extended the scope of inspiration to an institutional level. Her hard work towards the advancement of women in science both honors and champions the work done by Herschel.

It is this tireless spirit of scientific rigor that binds the legacies of these two juggernauts of astronomical accomplishment. These women paved the way for the ongoing process of improving the lives of women interested in math and science. Female astronomers, astrophysicists, and mathematicians have since discovered planets, comets, stars, and nebulae. They have calculated problems of immense magnitude and posited theories of profound importance. Female programmers performed much of the legwork that sent the first humans to the surface of the moon. There is no telling the limit to which these women have impacted the field of science, showing that in spite of the lack of formal education, institutions, or representation, women have shown the tenacity to make discoveries about the known universe.

CHRONOLOGY

1750   Caroline Herschel is born in Hanover, Germany.

1772   Herschel moves to England to pursue a career in singing.

1781   William Herschel discovers the planet Uranus.

1783   Herschel discovers her first nebula.

1785   The Herschels begin construction on the 40-foot (12-meter) telescope.

1786   Herschel discovers her first comet with a Newtonian sweeper, becoming the first woman to submit a paper to the Royal Astronomical Society.

1787   Herschel is granted a salary for her work as William's assistant, marking the first time a woman had ever been paid in England for scientific work.

1788   Herschel discovers her second comet.

1790   Herschel discovers a third and fourth comet.

1791   Herschel's fifth comet is discovered.

1797   Herschel discovers her eighth and final comet, which is the sixth to be uniquely discovered by her.

1802   The Royal Astronomical Society publishes her catalog of over five hundred new observations.

1822   William Herschel dies at age eighty-three, and Caroline returns to Hanover where she spends the rest of her life.

1828   The Royal Astronomical Society awards Caroline Herschel the Gold Medal for her contributions to astronomy.

1846   Herschel is awarded the Gold Medal of Science by the King of Prussia for her work as an astronomer.

GLOSSARY

American Association for the Advancement of Women
Organization founded in part by Professor Maria Mitchell in 1896, which focused on women's suffrage and progress in academia.

Atlas Coelestis Astronomical reference text written by John Flamsteed noting the position of stars in the sky.

binary systems A system in which two celestial objects orbit around each other due to gravitational movements.

chromatic aberration Visual distortion caused by the failure of a refracting lens to focus all of the colors in the visible light spectrum to a singular focal point.

concave Curving inward like the interior of a circle.

convex Curving outward like the exterior of a circle.

Copernican Revolution A period of advancement in astronomy started by Nicolaus Copernicus that asserted the heliocentric model of the solar system.

double star An astronomical observation in which two stars appear to be close in proximity whether they are an optical illusion or an actual binary star system.

empirical Based on observation or experience.

epicycle Orbital pattern in which a body moves in circles as it revolves around a planet or star.

eyepiece The viewing lens of a telescope that concentrates light for an observer.

focal length Power of a reflector or lens to focus light to a single point based on the distance away from the surface of the refractive or reflective device.

gnomon Triangular part of a sundial that casts a shadow on its face.

heliocentric Viewing the sun as being at the center of the solar system.

lunisolar calendar A calendar used by astronomers in many cultures that documents both lunar phase and the position of Earth relative to the sun.

meridian Concept used by astronomers to describe a theoretical circle around Earth that runs vertically through both the north and south poles.

misogyny Dislike of or contempt for women.

Miss Mitchell's Comet Telescopic comet discovered by Maria Mitchell in 1847, which won her the King of Denmark's Gold Medal.

nebulae Collections of gas and dust in space visible from the fluorescence caused by nearby stars and galaxies.

Newtonian sweeper A version of a reflective telescope pioneered by Sir Isaac Newton in which the focal point is reflected by an angled mirror for ease of observation.

optical double Illusion in which two stars are perceived to be close together upon observation due to their positions relative to Earth.

parabolic mirror Curved reflective surface used to collect and focus light for use in telescopes and other optical instruments.

parallax Difference in the perceived relative distance of objects based on a shift in observational vantage point.

peer review Process used in scientific journals and publications to verify discoveries and studies by recreating the conditions of a test.

postwagon A horse-drawn wagon.

reflector An optical telescope that uses mirrors to direct and concentrate light.

refractor A lens that causes refraction, or the bending of a lightwave.

retrograde movement Phenomenon in which a body orbits around another in the opposite direction of its rotation around an axis.

Royal Astronomical Society Organization founded in Britain in 1820 for the advancement of the field of astronomy sponsored by the British monarchy.

spherical aberration Optical distortion caused by the difference in focused light from the center of a lens or reflector out to its edges.

stereoscope A device that takes two photographs of the same object at slightly different angles; when the photographs are combined, it provides a deeper view of the object.

sunspots Dark spots of lower temperature on the surface of the sun caused by electromagnetic forces.

sweeping Methodical process of surveying the sky for astronomical observations by moving in columns.

theory of homocentric spheres Theory posited by Greek astronomers in which the solar system was described in terms of a series of perfect circles with the earth at its center.

three body problem Astronomical investigation on the nature of orbital patterns in a system which has three or more massive bodies.

transit of Venus Phenomenon in which Venus can be observed traveling between the Earth and the Sun; used to calculate a number of different relationships in astronomy.

triangulation Trigonometric calculation of distance by observing an object from two or more vantage points.

FURTHER INFORMATION

BOOKS

Bernardi, Gabriella. *The Unforgotten Sisters: Female Astronomers and Scientists Before Caroline Herschel.* New York: Springer Praxis Books, 2016.

Hoskin, Michael. *Discoverers of the Universe: William and Caroline Herschel.* Princeton, NJ: Princeton University Press, 2011.

Lemonick, Michael. *The Georgian Star: How William and Caroline Herschel Revolutionized Our Understanding of the Cosmos (Great Discoveries).* New York: W. W. Norton & Company, 2009.

WEBSITES

Astronomical Society of the Pacific's "Women in Astronomy: An Introductory Research Guide"

http://www.astrosociety.org/education/astronomy-resource-guides/women-in-astronomy-an-introductory-resource-guide

This website hosts an extensive collection of resources and profiles on female astronomers throughout history and includes a collection of contemporary women in astronomy with listed accomplishments.

The Maria Mitchell Association

http://www.mariamitchell.org

This is the official website of the Nantucket Science Center, dedicated to the celebrated astronomer Maria Mitchell. It contains links for archives of Mitchell's work and information about the galleries and exhibits.

Women in Astronomy Blog

http://womeninastronomy.blogspot.com

This website offers a collection of blog posts written by women currently working in the field of astronomy; topics range from astronomical discoveries to modern obstacles for women in science.

VIDEOS

Emily Winterburn Discusses Caroline Herschel's 1787 account of a new comet

https://www.youtube.com/watch?v=ocGHWf1sX_Q

In this interview, astronomical historian Emily Winterburn speaks about the significance of Caroline Herschel's contributions.

The Georgian Star: How William and Caroline Herschel Invented Modern Astronomy

https://www.youtube.com/watch?v=gkSXjpBQov0

In this lecture for the Royal Society, astronomical historian Michael Lemonick explains the impact of the Herschels on the field of astronomy.

BIBLIOGRAPHY

"Astronomy in the 18th Century, Longitude, Fuzzy Blobs and the Astronomer's Drinking Song." Cosmicelk.com. Accessed August 21, 2016. http://www.cosmicelk.net/astronomy18c.htm.

Editors of Encyclopedia Britannica. "Caroline Lucretia Herschel." Chicago, IL. Encyclopædia Britannica, Inc., 2016.

Evans, James and Michael Wulf Friedlander. "Astronomy." Chicago, IL. Encyclopædia Britannica, Inc., 2015.

Herschel, Caroline. "An Account of a New Comet. In a Letter from Miss Caroline Herschel to Charles Blagden, M. D. Sec. R. S." Volume 77 of *Philosophical Transactions of the Royal Society of London*, pp. 1-3. 1787.

———. "An Account of the Discovery of a Comet. In a Letter from Miss Caroline Herschel to Joseph Planta, Esq. Sec. R. S." Volume 84 of *Philosophical Transactions of the Royal Society of London*. p. 1. 1794.

———. *Memoir and Correspondence of Caroline Herschel.* Cambridge, England: Cambridge University Press, 2010.

Hoskin, Michael. *Caroline Herschel: Princess Of The New Heavens.* Sagamore Beach, MA: Science History Publications, 2013.

Kellermann, Kenneth I. and B.L. Klock. "Telescope." Chicago, IL. Encyclopædia Britannica, Inc., 2016.

"She Is an Astronomer." Accessed August 21, 2016. www. sheisanastronomer.org.

Shuttleworth, Martyn. "Ancient Astronomy, Science and the Ancient Greeks." Explorable.com. Accessed August 15, 2016. www. explorable.com/greek-astronomy.

Winterburn, Emily. "Learned Modesty and the First Lady's Comet: A Commentary on Caroline Herschel (1787) 'An Account of a New Comet'." *Philosophical Transactions of The Royal Society of Astronomy*, Volume 373 (2015). Accessed August 3, 2016. dx.doi. org/10.1098/rsta.2014.0210.

Zeilinski, Sarah. "Caroline Herschel, Assistant or Astronomer?" *Smithsonian Magazine*, December 8, 2010. http://www. smithsonianmag.com/science-nature/caroline-herschel-assistant-or-astronomer-39807005/?no-ist.

INDEX

Page numbers in **boldface** are illustrations. Entries in **boldface** are glossary terms.

ABOUT THE AUTHOR

Kevin McCombs has a bachelor's degree in philosophy and music from New College of Florida. He works full-time as a research and development technician at a Jacksonville-based drone company. In his free time, he volunteers with a non-profit and teaches robotics and other STEM skills to grade-school students. Through music, science, and hands-on skills, he seeks to help students find their passions in life.